Chancel

Vestry.

Pulpit

Reading Desk

Steeple.

Richd Brownlow   Jonathan   Knowles   Daniel   Markinfield   Wm

Joseph Wood   William Turner   John Dodd   Ann Roscoe   James

Breadth   Breadth   Breadths   Breadth

Henry Nightingale   David Marsden   Giles Timothy   Jno Greenhalgh   Thos Longworth   John Thornley

Thos Kirrn   Robert Lucas Manchester   Philip

John Hunter   John Walker   James Justice   John Fairhurst   Michael Hopkinson   Cockshaw Seward

To the Poor   John   Hopwood   Town   Isak Brushwide   Mr Ringway

Dakins   Dakins   Gartside   Agncolor   Robt Whitelegg   John Peak

John Longworth   James Pendlebury   Thos Marion   Robert   James Hart   Samuel Stansford   Richard Whitelegg

Edward Hazel   John Curtis   Taylors   Paul Bartholomew   W Hoozlh   John Mason   Richard Pilkington   Peter Hart

Wm Witley   George Multrem   John Norres   Elias Hart

John Pendlebury   Mary Morris   Henry Cecil

Roger Hart   Wm Hart

Breadth   Breadths   Breadth

MORE ABOUT HORWICH

by
M. D. Smith
in collaboration with E. M. Brownlow

Lee Lane, Horwich. Circa 1905. The coal delivery wagon is opposite the top of Julia Street outside the premises of H. Unsworth.

Wyre Publishing
North Villas, Garstang Road, St. Michael's on Wyre, Lancashire, PR3 0TE

First Published 1999
Copyright © 1999 M. D. Smith.

ISBN:0-9526187-4-5

ACKNOWLEDGEMENTS

I wish to thank most sincerely all those people who have in any way assisted in the completion of this work, particularly those whose names appear below :-

Doris Adamson
Jill. M. Aldersley
Joan Birchall
Edward Brownlow
Fred Brownlow
George Bush
Gladys Calvert (deceased)
Arthur and Gwen Clare
Albert Clayton
Geoffrey Drinkwater
Beris Foy
John Garrity
Canon Dennis Gatenby
Arthur Green
Gordon and Susan Kay
Paul Barry Mason
Brenda Mitchell
Cynthia Pearcy
Norman Pendlebury
Norman Carlton Slark
Eric Stuchbury
Mary Yates
Bolton Evening News
Horwich Town Council
Elsie Whittaker

Typesetting by Highlight Type Bureau Ltd, Bradford.
Printed by The Amadeus Press Ltd, Huddersfield.

Lee Lane, Horwich. *1902. (Photograph opposite page)*
The occasion for the procession pictured is the Coronation of King Edward VII. The horse drawn vehicle was used as a 'Black Maria' / Ambulance / Fever Wagon and was stored behind the Public Hall. The wagon was presented to Horwich Urban District Council on the 25th April 1899 by the local police. It was built at a cost of £124 by Messrs Wilson and Stockall of Bury. A silver plate on the side of the vehicle bore the inscription - "Presented to the inhabitants of Horwich by the members of the Bolton Division, Lancashire County Constabulary". The cost was met by donations and the proceeds of a football match played at Horwich on the 14th December 1898 between the County Police and Horwich tradesmen. The ambulance could carry two injured persons in a recumbent position, and was specially constructed to avoid all jolting or unsteady movement. Colonel Moorsom, the County Chief Constable, made the presentation on the bowling green behind the Public Hall and this was followed by a luncheon in the Public Hall provided by Mr Parr of the Bridge Hotel, Horwich. The ambulance remained in use until the 1920s when it was replaced by a motorised version but was held in reserve for a short time.

Church Street, Horwich. Circa 1905. The tramlines in the roadway make it possible to date this photograph because the route was only used between 1900 and 1907. On the extreme right is the Bridge Hotel next to Horwich Conservative Club with the statue of Benjamin Disraeli atop the frontal facade.

MORE ABOUT HORWICH

INTRODUCTION

The book, 'More about Horwich' is principally intended to supplement and update the earlier 'About Horwich', originally published in 1988. There are several reasons for not re-printing the original, the main ones being that much more information and photographs have become available since the initial publication; and advances in printing techniques mean that not only can existing photographs be more faithfully reproduced but even those poor quality images, not previously considered suitable, can be improved for inclusion.

Horwich has a rich and interesting history of which there is much information available. Indeed, it is not practical to include more than a cross-selection of material in existence. Although the present work contains some repetition in content, which is unavoidable; the major part of this publication comprises different textual and photographic inclusions from the earlier book.

As the third millennium approaches, it is appropriate to look back across the centuries over the paths already travelled. Evidence of pre-history has been discovered in the form of a Scandinavian axe-head, found in Tiger's Clough during 1946, which was subsequently dated to around 2500 B.C. A number of other finds also provide evidence of early inhabitants of the district including numerous flint arrowheads. The Pike Stones on Anglezarke Moor represent a Megalithic Tomb, whilst other ancient burial sites exist at Noon Hill and Winter Hill where tumulii have been identified. Excavation of these two mounds has established their use and a cinerary urn from one of the digs is held at Bolton Museum. At one time the Forest of Horwich, which was sixteen miles in circumference, represented one of the most valuable appendages of the Barony of Manchester. Several local inns still bear names associated with this period such as the Squirrel, the Bee Hive and the Greenwood. Roman soldiers are thought to have occupied a fortress at Blackrod from where several roads radiated including one which ran through Rivington to Mellor near Blackburn, which gave name to the property known as the Street.

Local historian, Thomas Hampson, recorded the history of Horwich which was published in 1883 and chronicles events until that date. What was not known to Mr. Hampson at the time was that the Lancashire and Yorkshire Railway Company were looking for a suitable site on which to build a locomotive works. Eventually, the Company was successful in bidding for land in Horwich and development of Horwich Locomotive Works commenced in earnest. Village life was shattered with the arrival of the works, the population rising more than threefold from 3,761 persons in the 1881 Census to 12,850 residents in a relatively short time span. Property development increased proportionately, resulting in the upgrade of Horwich to township status. Sadly, the locomotive works closed on the 31st December 1983, although the buildings still exist and many are presently used by various business concerns. The latest development in Horwich is the Middlebrook complex which contains a myriad of shops, a multi-screen cinema and hotels. In addition, the Reebok Stadium has been erected nearby which is the new home to Bolton Wanderers Football Club. A railway station has also been opened to service the football ground.

In the following pages it is proposed to look back over the last hundred years or so of Horwich history using photographs and documents to illustrate the past. One pleasing aspect of this type of approach is that it makes the point that everyone is equally important in the story and the content is re-assuring in that by identifying with the individuals and familiar scenes depicted, perspective and meaning is added to our own lives.

M. D. Smith.
Adlington, Lancashire.
1999

Lee Lane, Horwich. Circa 1880. Ralph Hart's butchery, 39 Lee Lane, Horwich, stands to the left with a wooden canopy over the door and window. Ralph is standing leaning against the wall wearing his apron. John A. S. OXTON'S clothier and outfitters shop is on the extreme right of this early photograph.

TABLE OF CONTENTS

Mill Hole Cottage, Foxholes, Horwich. 1884.

ROCKHAVEN CASTLE

Richard Brownlow was born at Manor House, Wilderswood, in 1814, the son of Christopher Brownlow. He married the daughter of Mr. Lomax, a Bolton auctioneer, but there were no children of the marriage. Richard Brownlow was an attorney at law with a successful practice in the Bolton area, the main offices being in Bridge Street, Bolton. He owned a considerable amount of property and land in and around Horwich. When he moved into Rock Haven during 1840 he set about transforming the property with extensions and improvements. Eventually Rock Haven became known as Rockhaven Castle, principally due to the castellated parapets (fitted in the 1880s) which adorned the structure. Local people knew the building as "'TORNEY BROWNLOW'S CASTLE" from his profession as an attorney. Richard Brownlow had a great love for animals, particularly horses, and along with William Bennett, the owner of Wilderswood Mill, and a Mr. Munday of Preston; he was responsible for the foundation of Horwich races. Initially the annual horse races were staged near to Manor House where Blackrod Reservoir was once situated but which has since been re-filled for agricultural use. The inaugural race was run on the 22nd August 1837. The venue for the second season was switched to a site near to the Squirrel Hotel and Anderton Old Hall off Squirrel Lane and was staged on the 2nd August 1838. The final site for a racecourse was a purpose built track constructed on the banks of the River Douglas at Old Lords. Such was the popularity of the event at this time that it took three days to complete the programme of races. The registered racing colours of Richard Brownlow were blue with a white cap. He owned a horse named 'Luck's All' which won several races for him. The animal was eventually sold to Mr. William Henry Hornby of Blackburn and continued a successful racing life under the new name 'Now or Never'. The last Horwich Races took place on Thursday 5th August 1847. One cause for its demise was the amount of undesirables that the races attracted which were felt to constitute a danger to the town's morality. In addition to his interest in horse racing, Richard Brownlow was a staunch churchgoer and was keenly active in local politics being at one time vice-president of the local Conservative Party. Towards the end of his life he became something of a recluse which was partially due to suffering from a facial disfigurement caused by erysipelas. He did, however, occasionally host several functions at Rockhaven Castle but chose to wear a mask to cover his disfigurement while in attendance. His death occurred on the 19th June 1899 when he was 85 years of age. Rockhaven Castle was demolished in 1942. One of the reasons given was because it provided an ideal fixing point for enemy aircraft trying to disable the war effort at either Horwich Locomotive Works or Lostock De-Havilland Works. Some of the stone from the castle was used to build a bungalow in Lytham while the remainder was carried as ballast on grain ships travelling to America. At the present time the whole area around the castle has been afforested and it is difficult to visualise where this fine, architecturally striking, building once stood.

The popularity of Rockhaven Castle is evinced to some degree by the large number of post card views showing the residence. A number of these are reproduced below.

Rockhaven Castle with Brinks Row in the foreground. Circa 1920.

Rockhaven Castle. 1908. This interesting view shows the approach road and entrance to the castle.

Rockhaven Castle. Circa 1908. An antique dealer named Hignett, who had business premises in Prince's Arcade, Horwich, once occupied the castle. During his tenancy the glass conservatory on the left was opened to the public as a tea-room.

Rockhaven Castle. Circa 1912.

Rockhaven Castle. Circa 1920.

Rockhaven Castle. Circa 1920. Richard Smith of Wilderswood Farm is standing in front of the castle.

Rockhaven Castle. Circa 1920.

Rockhaven Castle. Circa 1920.

THE HORWICH FLOOD OF 1850

On Tuesday, 16th July 1850, the day broke with a promise of fine weather, following several weeks of unsettled climatic conditions. A number of people were in fact tempted to climb the Rivington hills to the watchtower on Rivington Pike in order to enjoy the views from this popular vantage point. As the day wore on the sky became ominously black and at about 3-o'clock in the afternoon a terrible storm broke.

Rain lashed down in torrents to the accompaniment of roaring thunder and sheet lightning. Such was the suddenness with which the weather broke that the ramblers on the Pike were urgently forced to seek shelter and there was some concern felt for the safety of the children because a number of them had wandered off to play.

Several water courses take their rise in the Rivington hills and situated along the banks of the streams which descend the hills into Horwich were many industrial premises, including two textile mills belonging to Mr. Bennett and his son, respectively; Fairbrother's Brickworks, and a bleachworks operated by Mr. Kay which was sited in Tiger's Clough on the boundary between Horwich and Rivington. The reason for positioning these factories on the banks of streams was that the waters powered water wheels, which provided the motive power for machinery at the various works.

Such was the force of the water descending the hills on that day in 1850 that roadways were washed away leaving cavities up to six feet in depth. The mine workings at Mr. Brownlow's collieries were inundated with water rendering them unworkable. The reservoir at Mr. Bennett Junior's mill was breached and the lower rooms of the factory were flooded to a depth of several feet; whilst machinery was dislodged and anything moveable was swept away. A similar fate befell Mr. Bennett Senior's mill situated further downstream.

Purl Brook burst its banks and flowed along Winter Hey Lane carrying many industrial and household items which had been sucked into the maelstrom of its floodwaters.

A large dam at Fairbrother's Brickworks was filled up with sediment washed down from the hills and the water wheel was so badly damaged that it never worked again.

Mr. Kay's Bleachworks were constructed near to a large dam in Tiger's Clough and he lived above the works, his bedroom window being no more than about two feet from the wall of the dam. The storm caused water to pour into the living quarters at the mill prompting an emergency evacuation. However, the Tiger's Inn, a beerhouse situated upstream from the mill, was totally unaffected. One effect of the floodwaters in Tiger's Clough was that it uncovered a vein of pyrites which has the appearance of gold and is commonly known as 'fool's gold'. A number of local colliers, on hearing of the potential for gold prospecting, examined the seam and soon realised, to their disappointment, what the mineral actually was.

Sharrock's Fold Farm then (1850) stood on the site where Horwich Locomotive Works was eventually built after 1885. On the day of the flood the farm, which was tenanted by John Shaw, contained several occupants. John Shaw was present in the farmhouse together with Alice Makinson, aged 14 years, who was employed as a domestic servant and Alice's mother. Ellen Longworth, who was younger than Alice and the daughter of a previous farm tenant, was also at the property along with three other men and a young boy. In view of the severity of the storm, the two young girls were advised to go into a corner of the kitchen for safety but, unfortunately, the house was struck by lightning at about half past seven in the evening.

Alice Makinson was hit by the lightning and killed outright. She appeared to have been struck on the shoulder, the charge passing through her body and splitting the sole of one of her clogs from the leather upper, on exit. Ellen Longworth was found on the floor nearby with a large flitch of bacon on top of her. The bacon had previously been suspended from the kitchen ceiling by a hook. Ellen was badly injured and died the following morning. The other persons in the farmhouse escaped without injury.

Amongst the effects of the storm were that two railway steam locomotives passing through Horwich on the Bolton to Preston line had their boiler fires put out stranding them for over two hours. Kiln fires at the brickworks (later worked by Andrew Peak) were also swamped. A house in Lathom Row was struck by lightning resulting in a young man at the address being stunned but otherwise uninjured. Lightning also killed a colt out in the fields at Wilderswood.

Brinks Pit at Blackrod had its boilerhouse flooded and two men engaged in sinking a shaft were plunged into water when the level rose thirty feet. One of the men was drowned while the second managed to cling to a piece of timber until he was rescued many hours later.

As the floodwaters subsided, the clean-up operation began in earnest. The cost of the damage was astronomical. For example, Wilderswood Mills suffered damage estimated at £1,000 - a veritable fortune in those days. Other industrial concerns were so badly affected by the flood waters that they were forced to close. Much hardship was caused to the families who lost their livelihood as a result of the devastating flood.

Anderton Mill. 1904. The mill, which was demolished early this century, stood near to Anderton Old Hall by the River Douglas.

Anderton Waterfall on the River Douglas between Anderton
Lane and Crown Lane.

FARMSTEADS, COTTAGES, ETC.

WILDERSWOOD FARM

*Oak Villa, Horwich. Circa 1900. Oak Villa is presently known as Wilderswood Farm
and it stands near to the site of what was once the Blackrod reservoir.*

*Mr. Robert Smith photographed in front of Oak Villa, Horwich.
Circa 1900.*

Wilderswood Farm. Circa 1950. Haytime at Wilderswood Farm, Horwich; Brinks Row Cottages are in the background but Rockhaven Castle has been demolished.

Wilderswood Farm. Circa 1950.

DULSON'S FARM

Dulson's Farm, Bolton Fold, Horwich. 1962.

DICKINSON'S FARM

Dickinson's Farm, Vale Avenue, Horwich. Circa 1904. Hilton housing estate was subsequently developed on the farm land.

NEW CHAPEL POULTRY FARM

Mr. H. Whalley was the proprietor of New Chapel Poultry Farm which was also known as Chapel-in-the-Fields Poultry Farm. Brazley Avenue is the crescent of housing on the left. Claypool Estate was developed on the site of the farm.

HODGKINSON FOLD FARM, HORWICH

Horwich Parish Church Tower can be seen left of centre.

Rivington Pike Tower can be seen in the background.

HIGHER MEADOWS FARM

Higher Meadows Farm, Horwich. Circa 1910.

HARPER'S FARM

Harper's Farm, Wilderswood. Circa 1900.

BRINKS ROW COTTAGES

Brinks Row Cottages. 1900. These stone cottages are thought to date from 1759, which date was found carved on a stone during building alterations carried out this century. They have provided accommodation for weavers, miners and quarrymen over the years being situated in an area rich with underlying mineral resources. Mr. Finch, the one time owner of Pilkington Delph on Horwich Moor, lived at the cottage on the extreme left.

FOXHOLES, HORWICH

Foxholes Road, Horwich. Circa 1920.

Foxholes House, Horwich. Circa 1910. Foxholes House was the home of the Mason family for over a century. They were descendants of the Lords Willoughby of Parham, and owned extensive property in the district. The last members of this family to occupy the house were three spinster sisters, Elizabeth, Mary and Anne Mason. Anne was the last to die, in 190^ when the gross amount of her estate was valued at £22,828.

STOCKS COTTAGE, FLEET STREET, HORWICH

An attractive early view of Stocks Cottage, Fleet Street, Horwich. 1903.

Stocks Cottage was situated on the Stocks Estate and Richard Pilkington is recorded as the resident from 1761 until 1796. The Stocks Estate was purchased by the Ridgway family in 1803. The property was finally demolished during 1911.

HART'S HOUSES

Hart's Houses from Foxholes, with Rockhaven Castle in the background (right). Circa 1910.

MILL HOLE COTTAGE

These two views of Mill Hole Cottage were taken early this century.

HORWICH PUBLIC HALL

Peter Martin of the 'Street', Heath Charnock, funded the building of Horwich Public Hall on Lee Lane, Horwich, during 1878. It was intended as a social centre where local people could find ample means of spending a pleasant evening away from the public house. Conditions attached to the provision of the Hall were that it should not be used for denominational purposes, but be governed by a representative committee to be revised every five or seven years; and beverages other than intoxicants might be procured.

The public hall was officially opened on the 2nd April 1879, but Peter Martin only survived the ceremony by a few months, his death occurring on the 12th July 1879. His widow, Mrs Mary Tetlow Martin, eventually presented the building for the town's use in 1882 in accordance with what she believed would have been the wishes of her late husband and her late daughter, Mary Alice Martin, had they been living. Mrs Martin died at 'The Street' on the 22nd December 1893.

In connection with Queen Victoria's Golden Jubilee of 1887 a scheme was promoted in conjunction with Horwich Local Board for the provision of a 'free' lending library. A room was granted for use in the Public Hall and equipped for use as a library at a cost of £115-17s-9d, which included the cost of the books. The library was officially opened on the 14th November 1887.

Horwich Public Hall, Lee Lane, Horwich. Circa 1905.
The building is described in Thomas Hampson's 'History of Horwich' (1883) as follows:- "The Hall covers an area of 32 superficial yards, and the offices, stables and outbuildings cover a further space of 136 yards. The bowling green is 52 yards by 36. The view from the outside is delightful, the hills forming a kind of background to a lovely landscape. The general style of the building is of the Gothic design, Elizabethan type. The front is extremely attractive, being of pressed brick, relieved by a terra cotta tracery; the apex being of Yorkshire stone. The interior of the building is in keeping with its outward aspect, the handsome staircase of polished pitch pine, together with the other appointments, being most harmonious. On the ground floor is the billiard room, reading rooms, chess and draughts room and coffee room, over which is a large assembly room of 1,505 square feet, the most striking feature of the building, perhaps, being the turret, surmounted by a weather vane, from which project the points of the compass."

Aerial view of Horwich Town Centre. 1988. (Bolton Evening News Photograph.) Horwich Public Hall stands just to the right of centre and can be identified with the bowling green behind. Chorley New Road runs along the bottom of the photograph.

Close-up view of Horwich Public Hall. Circa 1905. The 'free' lending library is on the left of the building on the corner. Three stone cottages stood on the right of the Hall one of which was used as a Police Station in the 1850's. The cottages were eventually demolished and replaced with a lawned area.

Horwich Public Hall, Lee Lane, Horwich. Circa 1915.

Farnham Slade Horwich U. D. C, South Ward Candidate, 1907

Councillor Eileen Kay hands over the Chairmanship of Horwich U. D. C to Alan Oakley. 1972

Horwich U. D. C Councillors at Horwich Leisure Centre1975. Horwich Leisure Centre was opened by H. R. H. Princess Anne on the 18th March 1975. Present at the Centre are
(Left to Right)
Jim Mc Burnie, Albert Radcliffe, Walter Taylor, Ellis Dobson, Eileen Kay, Alan Oakley, Desmond Smith (Chairman), member of the centre staff, Betty McCracken, Peter Hewitt, Kenneth Sale and Gerald Hind.

Lee Lane, Horwich. 1990.

*Beside the Public Hall, where cottages once stood, is this well-kept garden area
with the town's coat-of-arms emblazoned in flowers.*

HORWICH PARISH CHURCH

Holy Trinity Parish Church, Horwich. Circa 1910.

During 1879 a series of historical notes on Horwich and its Parish Church appeared in the Bolton Chronicle. Jas. A. Partington, a local historian of 169 Crown Lane, Horwich, carefully preserved the relevant newspaper cuttings until his death in August 1943 when they were handed over to Samuel Drinkwater. Since this time they have been safely kept by the Drinkwater family. The articles contain much of interest concerning the Church, which is summarised below: -

In 1565 the Commissioners for Removing Superstitious Ornaments informed the Bishop of Chester that they had "taken away from Horwich Chapel vestment, albe, altar-cloth, corporasse, and other idolatrous gear" from which it appears that the minister was felt to be leaning towards the teaching of Catholicism.

Mr. Henry Pendlebury, B.A., described as a painful, godly, preaching minister, preached at Horwich Chapel during 1650. No salary was paid and the minister had to rely on the benevolence of the inhabitants.

In the early years of the 18th Century the Revd. James Rothwell, vicar of the mother church at Deane, Bolton, communicated his concerns regarding Horwich Chapel to the Bishop of Chester in a letter which was initially addressed to the Revd. Dr. Wroe, Warden of Manchester. (The full text of the letter is included at Appendix 1.)

Protracted litigation ensued with the result that, in 1724, by a decree of the Commissioners for Charitable Uses, £200 was recovered, together with £80 for arrears of interest, from the Dissenters, in whose hands the chapel money was lodged, but most of the £80 was used to defray the charges of the suit and to pay the curate who officiated, so that £200 remained only of the stock.

The earliest church register dates back to 1660, the year of the Restoration of Charles II. There are only three entries for this year, namely the baptism of William Gorton, son of Giles Gorton, and two other children whose names are difficult to decipher with any degree of certainty. The first recorded burial is that of Esther Greenhalgh in 1662.

Interior view of Horwich Parish Church. Circa 1895. Box pews comprised the seating for the church until the 1950's. A chancel was added in 1903 in memory of Reverend Pigot who was the incumbent at Horwich from 1853 until 1901.

This view shows the perspective of Horwich Parish Church interior from the altar. The beautiful old pipe organ towers above the entrance door and the baptismal font is in the centre of the aisle. Circa 1895.

On the 29th December 1853, Horwich Chapel was constituted a separate ecclesiastical district, its mother church being up to that time the venerable sacred pile at Deane, the Vicar of which parish is patron of the living of Horwich.

Reverend Henry Pendlebury, M.A., who was mentioned as preaching at Horwich Chapel in 1650, was ejected from the Ministry through the Act of Uniformity in 1662. However, it appears that the Revd. James Walton was also ejected as Minister of Horwich Chapel about the same time. Dr. Calamy wrote: - "It is certain he (Rev Walton) was some time minister of this chapel (Horwich), which is in Deane Parish, but it is doubtful whether he was ejected here or at Shaw, near Oldham. He was provided with no sustenance when ejected, and had several children. He died in 1664, aged 64 years. He was a laborious, faithful minister".

The oldest dated gravestone in Horwich Chapel graveyard (in 1879) was that belonging to the family of Andrew Peak. At the top of the gravestone were the initials M. H. and the date 1648. It is not known who this person was because the parish registers only commenced in 1660. Beneath the initials was the following inscription:
"To the memory of James Peak, son of John and Alice Peak, of Horwich, who died July 20th, 1779, aged 29". There is little doubt that interments took place at Horwich Chapel prior to 1648.

In the 1879 newspaper article, reference is made to a most remarkable and singular monument standing in Horwich churchyard. The monument referred to is the Willoughby Monument and is described as being of large size, embellished with the Arms of the Barons Willoughby, neatly blazoned. There are seven small shields below, blazoned, containing the arms of those who have intermarried with the de-Parhams, viz.: - Bridgewaters, Egertons, Davenports, Halliwells, Fishers, Shaws and others. The following is the substance of the inscription: - "In memory of Thomas, the eleventh Lord Willoughby, of Parham in Suffolk, of Adlington, and Shaw Place, in the County Palatine of Lancaster, who died February 20th, 1691, aged 89. Also Eleanor Lady Willoughby, who died in 1665, aged 67; and Hugh, their eldest son, twelfth Lord Willoughby, who died in June 1712, aged 75, also Lady Honora, his second wife, eldest daughter of Lord Leigh of Stoneleigh Abbey, and relict of Sir William Egerton, of Worsley, Knight of the Bath, second son of John, Earl of Bridgewater, and his Countess, Elizabeth, daughter of his Grace the Duke of Newcastle: she died in 1830, aged 77, and was endeared to all who knew her, by every virtuous quality and purity of life, and beloved for amenity of manners, loving to all whom she was acquainted with, devout and truly religious, and full of Christian charity and benevolence, which was evinced at her favourite retreat, Worsley Hall".

It seems that the monument in Horwich churchyard gradually deteriorated and what eventually happened to it is not known.

Apparently, Mr. John Shaw of Rivington commissioned a replica of the Willoughby Monument in 1845 which was to be placed in Rivington Chapel. A firm in Wigan undertook the commission and the finished memorial was delivered to Rivington by horse and cart.

On the 18th October 1936, Mr. George Nuttall Shawcross, of Dean Wood House, Rivington, copied the letter, reproduced below, which refers to the transaction:

Wigan 20th December 1845.

Dear Sir,

I beg to inform you that the Armorial bearings are nearly finished and the artist, Mr. Magnall tells me that he will have them at my house complete in about a fortnight, the parts that I have seen are splendid. He is preparing the Arms of Willoughby, Whittle, Halliwell, Leigh, Egerton, Davenport - the Crown and Saracen's Head for the top and then the quarters, then again, and place them along with his Lordship's at the bottom, which he pledges to have at my house complete Friday week. The sculptor is also at work placing the inscription upon the stone, which is expected to be complete in about a fortnight.

I am, dear Sir, yours truly,
(Signed)   Cha's Leigh.

Some of the communion plate is described including one silver service engraved on the chalice of which are the words "From an oratorio 1781". Upon the alms dish appears the legend, "The gift of the Rev. John Parker, of Breightmet, to Horwich Church, 1782". The tankard or wine jug is inscribed, "The gift of the Rev. Henry Offley Wright, to Horwich Chapel 1782". A second silver communion service was presented by Joseph Ridgway, Esq., of Ridgmont.

On the walls of the church are two large paintings of the Ridgway family crest and that of the Willoughbys. Memorial tablets include the following: -
(1) Sacred to the memory of Thomas Ridgway, Esq., of Wallsuches, in this township, who died 30th August, 1816, aged 77; also Mary his wife, who died 23rd April 1803, aged 63. They were both interred at the Parish Church, Bolton "Blessed are the dead which die in the Lord".

(2) To the memory of Charles Howarth, of Moor Platt, Horwich, whose strict integrity, uprightness, and warm heart endeared him in life to all who knew him. Born August 19th 1805; died May 29th, 1860. This tribute of regard is erected to his memory by a few of his intimate friends.

Moor Platt, Horwich. Circa 1890.

(3) To the memory of the Revd. Samuel Johnson, M.A., for 34 years vicar of Atherton, Lancashire, who died August 13, 1873, at Upton Helions, Devon, aged 77. His father was Vicar of Horwich.

(4) To the memory of William Longworth, and his wife, erected by their sons, John and Nathaniel.

A large stained glass window, situated near to one of the Ridgway pews, which occupy the spaces at each side of the chancel bears the following inscription underneath, "In memory of Christopher Howarth, of Colemans, in this parish, who died 3rd June, 1874, aged 67 years. This window was erected in affectionate remembrance by his widow, 1874".

Horwich Parish Church, as it stands today, was originally built by Parliamentary grant and subscription, the first stone being laid by Joseph Ridgway, Esq., of Ridgmont, on the 21st May, 1830. The Ridgway family owned Wallsuches Bleachworks in Horwich and made many benefactions to the district.

Etching of Ridgmont House, home of the Ridgway family who were the owners of Wallsuches Bleachworks. 1846.

Aerial view of Wallsuches Bleachworks, Horwich. Circa 1935.

Ridgmont House, 1979. The home of the Ridgways has now been converted for use by the various Horwich Lodges of Free and Accepted Masons.

The present building is at least the third place of worship to be erected on the site. John Longworth, who had a bleachworks in Horwich, possessed an old parchment which contained the original faculty for taking down the first known Horwich Chapel and erecting the second. (The full text of this document is reproduced at Appendix 2.)

Within the records held at the church are plans of the present church and the previous chapel. A pencil drawing also exists of the second chapel, purported to have been sketched by the incumbent, David Hewitt, who officiated at Horwich Parish Church from 1826 until 1852. There is no other information on the first chapel other than a drawing of the entrance done in 1574.

There is a story that Reverend Hewitt and Joseph Ridgway did not enjoy a friendly relationship. Thomas Hampson, in his book, the History of Horwich, makes the following veiled reference to their antipathy when commenting on the various provisions of Joseph Ridgway's will. (See Appendix 3.) In accordance with the provisions of this will, a neat board at the entrance of the church gives the amount available yearly to the church officers. For ten years the more important and directly beneficial clauses of the "will" were inoperative, as only in 1852 did Reverend David Hewitt resign the incumbency. The why and wherefore of Mr. Ridgway's antipathy to the rev. gentleman is not to our purpose to enquire, sufficient is it to say that Horwich Church is perhaps somewhat incongruously made to be made more or less a heraldic monument of the Ridgway family, and perhaps an enquiry might lead to the conclusion that the proscribed clergyman suffered through an unavoidable clash in defence of ecclesiastical rights and privileges."

Several stories exist as to the cause of the ill-feelings between the two men. It has been suggested that David Hewitt once forbade Joseph Ridgway to take part in a procession of senior church dignitaries. Another story exists that Reverend Hewitt, who lived at the manse in Fleet Street, Horwich, saw fit to complain of noisy parties at Ridgmont, with the result that Joseph Ridgway mounded up earth between the two properties to form a hill which became known locally as 'the hill of spite'. A statue of a racehorse was placed atop the hill. The animal belonged to the Ridgway stable and was named Colonel Jeffrey. It was destroyed by drunken vandals in 1859.

Part of the Ridgway family crest contains the figure of a camel and yet another explanation for the bad blood between the two men concerns a sermon preached by Reverend Hewitt based upon the Book of Matthew, Chapter 19, verses 23 and 24, which state:-
Vs. 23. Then said Jesus unto his disciples, verily I say unto you, That a rich man shall hardly enter into the kingdom of heaven.

Vs. 24. And again I say unto you, It is easier for a camel to go through the eye of a needle than for a rich man to enter the kingdom of God.

Whatever Reverend Hewitt intended in selecting this text, Joseph Ridgway took the meaning as a personal affront and any remaining good will between the two men was lost.

The Ridgway family crest which stands against the wall in Horwich Parish Church grounds.

Right: The Ridgway family vault.

Below left: Joseph Ridgway of Ridgmont, Horwich. (From an oil painting) Joseph Ridgway died at Leamington on the 26th June 1842, aged 77 years, and was buried in the family vault at Horwich Church on the 6th July 1842.

Below right: Rev. David Hewitt, M.A., Vicar of Horwich 1826 - 1852.

Pencil sketch of the Second Church. By Rev. D. Hewitt. Vicar. About 1825.

CLERGY AT HORWICH

A list of Clergy at Horwich Church appears on page 45 of Hampson's History of Horwich, which reads:-

Oct	1521	Edward Tempest
	1650	Henry Pendlebury
	1662	James Walton
Dec	1731	Robert Harvey
	1749	John Norcross
	1788	Samuel Johnson, ob. 13 Mar., 1826
	1826	David Hewitt
	1853	Henry Septimus Pigot, M.A.

The Bolton and District Family History Society compiled the following chronological list of incumbents at Horwich Church. (1985)

HOLY TRINITY CHURCH

MINISTERS AT HORWICH CHAPEL.

	Circa	1565	Peter Mackinson.
	Circa	1621	Edward Tempest.
	Circa	1637	Henry Whittle.
	Circa	1641 - 1648	James Walton.
		1650 - 1651	Henry Pendlebury. B.A.
	Circa	1656 - 1657	John Isherwood. B.A.
	OCC.	1671	John Barton.
		1702 - 1720	John Horobin. B.A.
		1720 - 1724	Nathan Pierpoint. B.A.
		1724 - 1731	Robert Harvey. B.A.
		1732 - 1765	John Norcross. B.A. (Senior)
2nd Chapel		1765 - 1788	John Norcross. B.A. (Junior)
		1788 - 1826	Samuel Johnson. M.A.
Church		1826 - 1853	David Hewitt. B.A.
		1853 - 1901	Henry Septimus Pigot. M.A.
		1901 - 1908	G.H.St. P. Garrett. M.A. B.D.
		1908 - 1921	Samuel Shephard.
		1921 - 1923	Robert Jennings Cross. B.A.
		1923 - 1927	Robert C. Worsley. B.A.
		1927 - 1936	Thomas Backhouse. M.A.
		1936 - 1942	Fred Addison. M.A.
		1942 - 1953	Thomas Murray. S.Th.
		1953 - 1961	Douglas R. Michell. M.A.
		1962 - 1972	George V. H. Eliott. M.A.
		1972 -	Denis W. Gatenby. M.A.

There is doubt as to the identity of the minister at Horwich Chapel who was ejected during 1662 when the Act of Uniformity came into operation. In the 'Ejections of 1662', Baines records James Walton as the minister ejected at Horwich. The researches of the Bolton and District Family History Society show James Walton as officiating at Horwich Chapel from 1641 until 1648. Doctor Calmy comments that, "Mr. James Walton. It is certain he was sometime minister at this chapel (Horwich) which is in Deane Parish, but it is doubtful whether he was ejected here or at Shaw Chapel, near Oldham."

Horwich was created a separate parish during 1853, the same year that Henry Septimus Pigot took over as incumbent.

Rev. Henry Septimus Pigot. M.A.
Vicar of Horwich 1853 - 1901.

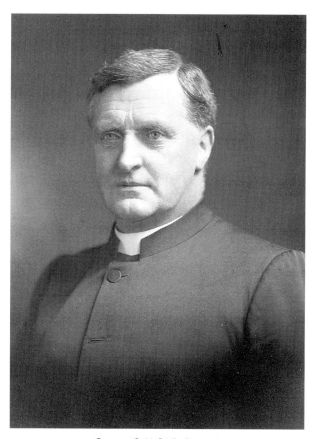

Canon G.H.St.P. Garrett.
Vicar of Horwich. 1901 - 1908.

Rev. Samuel Sheppard.
Vicar of Horwich. 1908 - 1921.

Rev. T. Murray. S.Th.
Vicar of Horwich. 1942 - 1953.

View of Church Street from Horwich Parish Church tower. Circa 1950.

VIEW FROM HORWICH PARISH CHURCH.

Wilderswood from the church tower. Circa 1920.

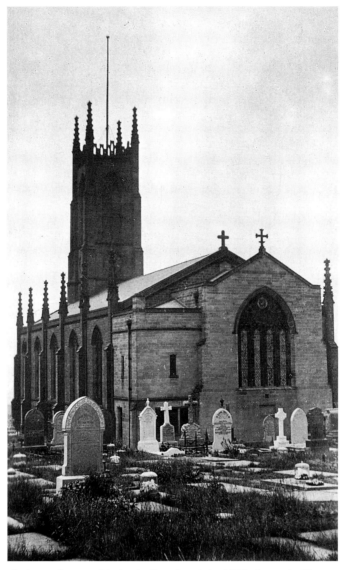

A chancel was added onto the church in 1903. It was built as a memorial to Reverend H. S. Pigot, M.A., incumbent from 1853 to 1901.

HORWICH PARISH CHURCH.

REV. CANON F. ADDISON, M.A., VICAR.
DESIGNATE OF HORWICH.

INTERIOR.

Promotional Calendar for a 1936 sale of work at Horwich Parish Church.

IN MY FATHER'S HOUSE THERE ARE MANY MANSIONS

Horwich is a town which caters for the members of several different religious denominations each of which has a rich and interesting past. It would best be served if a complete history of each place of worship could be provided but this is not a practical proposition as far as this work is concerned. Nevertheless, there follows a selection of material which shows the importance of religion in our everyday lives.

Holy Trinity Mission Church, Lord Street, Horwich. Circa 1900.

Holy Trinity Mission Church trip to Southport. Circa 1920.

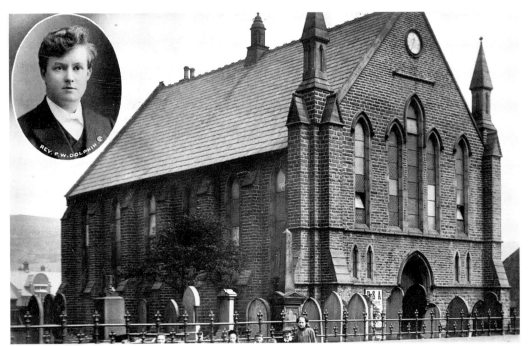

Lee Lane Congregational Chapel, Horwich. Circa 1900. This chapel, built in 1856, replaced an earlier place of worship. It was designed by Mr. George Woodhouse, Architect of Bolton. It was built of local stone and the cost, including the front and rear boundary walls, heating apparatus, levelling the ground and architect's charges, was £1,500. A Sunday school is recorded as being opened in 1789 under the inspection of Reverend Leonard Redmayne. The first authentic record of a day school was in 1814 when James Rothwell was schoolmaster but the school was probably in existence prior to this date.

Horwich Unitarian Free Church had its origin at a meeting held in the house of Mr. Jefferson, 51 Mary Street West on the 23rd October 1890. The possibility of establishing a Unitarian Church in Horwich was discussed with the unanimous meeting decision being in favour. Following enquiries and conferences a further meeting was held in Gunn's Refreshment Room, Chorley New Road, on the 10th of November 1890. The room was rented for services and an inaugural service was held on the 30th November 1890, attended by some 30 persons. After a short time it was learned that rooms at Gorton Fold, which had been previously used for religious services were to become vacant so the Unitarians made approaches to secure the rooms. Gorton Fold was eventually opened on the 22nd February 1892, the pulpit used being the gift of Essex Church, London. Eventually it was decided to build a new church and the memorial stone was laid on the 6th July 1895. The building opened on the 22nd February 1896.

John Riding, organist at Lee Congregational Chapel. Circa 1920.

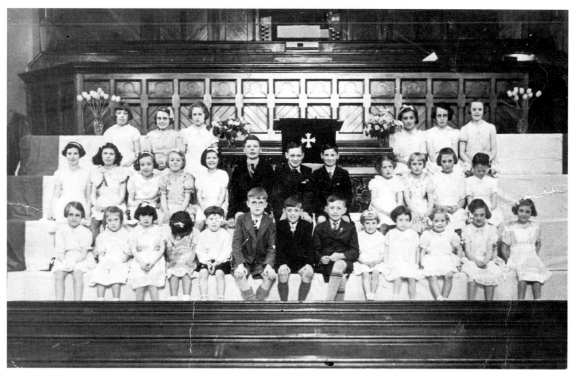

Victoria Wesleyan Chapel, Horwich. 1938.

Horwich Independent Methodist Bowling Club. Circa 1910.

St. Mary's R.C. Church, Chorley New Road,
Horwich. Circa 1930.

Interior view of St. Mary's R. C. Church,
Chorley New Road, Horwich. Circa 1930.

Wedding party outside St. Mary's
R.C. Church. Circa 1950.

May Queen ceremony inside St. Mary's R. C. Church. Circa 1950.

This photograph taken in the driveway of St. Mary's R.C. Church has the Horwich Spiritualist Church and Lyceum in the background.

Horwich Spiritualist Church and Lyceum, Horwich. Circa 1960.

The Manse, Chapel-in-the-Fields, Horwich. 1905.

New Chapel United Reformed Church, New Chapel Lane, Horwich. 1999.

Aenon Pentecostal Church, Chapel Street, Horwich. 1990.

Horwich Evangelical Church, Wright Street, Horwich. 1999.

Independent Methodist Church, Lee Lane, Horwich. 1999. The church was built to accommodate the rise in worshippers following the arrival of the locomotive works. The foundation stone laying ceremony took place on the 25th August 1906.

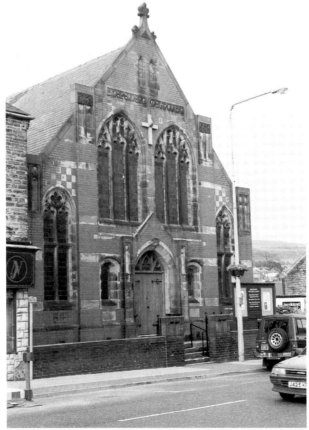

St. Elizabeth's Church, Claypool, Horwich. 1994.

THE SOUND OF BELLS

Whilst researching the history of the Holy Trinity Parish Church at Horwich it was my privilege to speak to Frederick William Brownlow whose family have long been connected with the church, in particular the ringing of the church bells. Fred was born in John Street, Horwich, on the 9th March 1904, and despite having passed his 90th birthday could still recall with amazing clarity events associated with the church. His grandfather's uncle, Richard Yates, was among the first bell-ringers at Horwich Parish Church in 1841, not long after it was first opened in 1830.

This Christening photograph of the Brownlow family was taken in George Street, Horwich, about 1905. Fred is the baby held by his mother, Amy. Ellen Brownlow, Fred's aunt, is on the extreme left and Polly Kirkman (nee Brownlow) on the extreme right. Alfred, George, Joe, Adam and Alexander Brownlow are left to right on the back row. The God-parents, Daniel and Jane, are seated behind their daughters.

Daniel Brownlow, who was Fred Brownlow's grandfather, died in 1924 aged 85 years and, at the time, was believed to be the oldest bell ringer in Lancashire. Apart from an eight year spell at Leyland Moss Side Church, Daniel remained at Horwich Parish Church until becoming seriously ill five weeks before his death. As a tribute to his services a muffled peal tribute was rung for Daniel Brownlow.

73 Years as a Bell-Ringer

Muffled Peel Tribute to Horwich Man

MR. D. BROWNLOW

When Mr. Daniel Brownlow, believed to be the oldest bell-ringer, in Lancashire, was interred at Horwich Parish Church, on Saturday, a muffled peel from the bells he had loved paid him a last homage.

Mr. Brownlow who was 85 years of age, "swung on the bell ropes" in Horwich Parish Church belfry before he could walk. As a boy his father gave him a thorough training in the bell-ringer's art, and at the age of 12 he accepted a bell at Leyland Moss Side Church. Eight years later he filled a vacancy at Horwich Parish Church, and was a regular ringer until he became ill about five weeks ago.

It was his proud boast that though approaching 90 he could climb the 52 steps to the belfry without a halt. His 73 years' service as a bell-ringer, 65 of which had been at the Horwich Church, is a record which has not been challenged.

In an address at the funeral service, the Rev. Canon Elsee, M.A. Vicar of St. George's, Bolton, referred to Mr. Brownlow's long service as a bell-ringer. Bell-ringers, said Canon Elsee, were church workers, and he had always been impressed by the comradeship which existed amongst them, which was real and strong.

On the re-building of Horwich Parish Church in 1830, Joseph Ridgway endowed the church with six bells. In 1913, the original bells were re-cast by Messrs John Taylor & Co., of Loughborough. Two smaller bells were added to the original peal making eight in total. The total cost of the operation was £400; £350 of which was raised by private subscription. Reverend Canon Chapman, B.D., Rural Dean, dedicated the bells in a short ceremony held in June 1913.

Fredrick William Brownlow commenced as a bell ringer at Horwich Parish Church in 1925. Until 1930 there were six bell ringers at Horwich Parish Church who were paid out of the Ridgway family bequest.

Holy Trinity Church
Horwich
Particulars of the ring of bells

Bell No.	Note	Diameter ft ins	Weight Cwt grs lbs
Treble	G	1 - 11¾	3 - 0 - 13
2	F#	2 - 0½	3 - 1 - 4
3	E	2 - 2½	3 - 3 - 21
4	D	2 - 4½	4 - 2 - 4
5	C	2 - 7¼	6 - 0 - 2
6	B	2 - 9	6 - 3 - 13
7	A	3 - 0½	9 - 0 - 18
8	G	3 - 5	12 - 3 - 13

The old ring of six recast and two trebles added completing the octave. New fittings and frame for eight bells.

John Taylor & Co.
Loughborough
1913

Mr Brownlow works the winding mechanism at Holy Trinity Parish Church.

It's time Fred had a rest

Mr **FRED BROWNLOW** has had time on his hands for the past 22 years – and his wife feels it's about time he had a rest.

This is not nearly so silly as it sounds. For during these years Mr Brownlow has been "custodian" of the clock at Holy Trinity Parish Church, across the road from his home in Church Street, Horwich.

Twice weekly he has to ascend 52 stone steps to the ringing chamber and then climb up a 20-rung ladder to wind up the clock.

The job of winding the weights, the heaviest of which is 10cwt, takes about 20 minutes to complete, and it is certainly no easy task.

"I don't mind doing it, but my wife says I am not getting any younger and it's about time I gave it a rest," said 65-years-old Mr Brownlow, who recently retired as a fitter from the British Railways Workshops at Horwich.

OBSOLETE

And the church council wholeheartedly agree with her. They want the clock, which for more than 230 years has recorded the time for the people of Horwich, to be installed with an electric winding apparatus.

The vicar, Canon G.V.H. Eliott, points out: "The winding up of large public clocks by hand is rapidly becoming as obsolete as the hand blowing of organs. All over the country these clocks are being electrified and soon there will be no hand clocks of this type left.

"The church council is conscious of the debt it owes to Mr Brownlow and realises it ought not to depend upon his good will in this matter indefinitely,"

Mr Eliott states that electrification of the apparatus would be £560. The problem is where to find the money.

The vicar says that recent expenses have exhausted church reserves and he is hopeful that one or more people may consider making a memorial gift for this purpose.

INSUFFICIENT

Joseph Ridgway, a benefactor of the church, many years ago left some money for the maintenance of the clock, but today it is no-where near sufficient for the purpose.

Mr Eliott adds: "The church clock is a permanent and prominent feature of our town. To ensure that it will continue to perform its function in the future would be a most useful service to both the church and the community and a fitting way of perpetuating the memory of a loved one".

FOOTNOTE: Several local authorities in the area, including Westhoughton, have made donations for a similar purpose. Perhaps Horwich Council may follow suit?

Newspaper report which appeared in The Journal on the 4th July 1969.

Fred Brownlow readies the flag on top of Horwich Parish Church tower. Circa 1960.

CHURCH ACTIVITIES, SPORT AND LEISURE
A MISCELLANY

First Harvest Rose Queen Festival at Horwich Parish Church. Circa 1950. The Queen is Rene Cocker and the crowner is Mrs. Murray, wife of the vicar. Mr. Wilf Tomkinson is officiating as Local Authority Chairman. The small girl on the left is Ruth Brownlow, daughter of Fred Brownlow the parish bell ringer.

A Dog Show held at Horwich Unitarian Chapel. Circa 1950.

STREET PARTIES

Winter Street, Horwich. 1935. Street party to celebrate the Silver Jubilee of King George V.

St. Anne's Road, Horwich. 1945. Street Party to celebrate Victory in Europe.

HORWICH URBAN
DISTRICT COUNCIL.

CORONATION

of Her Majesty

QUEEN ELIZABETH II

2nd JUNE, 1953

Programme of
Local Celebrations

Sunday, 31st May, 1953.

At the request of Her Majesty the Queen, Special Services are being held in **all** Churches on Sunday, the 31st May, 1953. The Chairman and Members of the Horwich Council and the Coronation Committee have been invited to attend the Special Service at the Parish Church and will assemble outside the Church a few minutes before the Service starts at 10-30 a.m.

Please note - there will be no Civic Procession on this occasion.

Tuesday, 2nd June, 1953.

1-45 p.m.

The Leigh British Legion Prize Band will assemble in front of the Public Hall and play the National Anthem and then parade along Lee Lane to the Crown and down Chorley New Road, along Ramsbottom Road to the Grundy Hill Football Field.

2-30 p.m.   On Grundy Hill Football Field.

Grand Coronation Sports organised by the Horwich R.M.I. Harriers and Athletic Club and the Horwich Cycling Club, will take place on the Grundy Hill Football Field

(by kind permission of the Railway Authorities).

School children aged between 6 and 15 years are competing, and prizes to a total value of £10 10s. 0d. have been given by the Coronation Committee.

In the Horwich Cycling Club Track Cycle Races, there are prizes to a total value of £6 0s. 0d., also given by the Coronation Committee.

The Prizes will be presented by the Chairman of the Council.

A separate programme, price 6d. on sale on the field, will give full details of these races, which will occupy approximately three hours.

Other attractions, including Remote Control Model Aeroplane Flying, releasing of Homing Pigeons, Fortune Telling, and other amusements, are being planned.

During the afternoon, the Band will be playing at frequent intervals.

Tuesday, 2nd June, 1953—continued.

6-45 p.m.

A Concert will be given by the Leigh British Legion Prize Band, and there will be open air dancing to the music of the Band until dusk.

Admission to the Field will be free of charge.

Refreshments will be available at moderate charges, and catering will be by Mr. William Salmon of Adlington.

Liquid refreshments will be obtainable on the field and will be catered for by Messrs. Greenall, Whitley & Co., Ltd., of St. Helens.

Ice Cream, supplied by Mr. J. Ferretti of Horwich, will also be available.

At Independent Methodist Sunday School
(Albert Street Entrance).
(by kind permission of the Leaders of the Church)

From 10-0 a.m. to 3-0 p.m.

Two Television Sets will be installed in the Independent Methodist Sunday School, Albert Street entrance, and Old Age Pensioners will be admitted to the school to watch the London Coronation Proceedings. T.V. Sets installed by Mr. Frank Abbott of Horwich.

On the Public Hall Bowling Green.
1-45 p.m.

A Bowling Tournament has been arranged by the Public Hall Bowling Club (Men's and Women's Sections) on the Public Hall Bowling Green, and two Cups (given by the Coronation Committee) will be awarded to the successful competitors. The Chairman of the Council will present the Cups.

Entry Fee 1/6d. - Entries to be handed to any member of the Committee not later than Saturday, the 30th May, 1953. All entry money to be given back in prizes.

Wednesday Evening, 3rd June, 1953.

On the R.M.I. Cricket Field.
6-30 p.m.

Cricket Match - C. Lawson's Eleven v. J. Fearnhead's Eleven.

Admission 6d.

Thursday Evening, 4th June, 1953.
At the Victoria Methodist Schoolroom.

7-30 p.m. (doors open 7-0 p.m.)

Horwich Schools Music Festival Concert.

Musical Director - J. E. A. Hinton, Esq., H.M.I.
Accompanist   - Landon S. Wood, Esq., L.R.A.M., A.T.C.L.

Admission 1/6d.

In addition to the foregoing festivities the Coronation is being celebrated as follows:-

(a) School Children:

All school children attending schools in Horwich will receive a souvenir cup and saucer and parties which have been provided by the Council will be held in every school on Wednesday, the 3rd June, 1953.

A few children in the town who are unable to attend any school either in Horwich or outside the district owing to a disability, although they are of school age, will be provided with a cup and saucer as a souvenir, also a monetary gift, which will be handed to their parents on Coronation Day.

(b) Old Age Pensioners:

All old age pensioners (Men of 65 years of age and over and Women of 60 years of age and over) will receive a gift of 2/6d. which will be handed to them in an envelope suitably endorsed, over the counter at the Post Office where they are usually paid their pension, on a pension day in the week prior to Coronation Day.

(c) National Service Men in a War Zone:

Men in H.M. Forces, who are serving in a war zone, i.e. Korea or Malaya, will receive a gift of £1 1s. 0d.

(d) Window Display Competition:

The Chamber of Trade is working in conjunction with the Horwich Carnival Committee in the organisation of a Window Display Competition, and it is hoped that a large number of traders will join in this Competition.

(e) Side Streets Decoration Competition:

The Coronation Committee are offering prizes for the best decorated side streets, and an advertisement, giving full details of this Competition has appeared in the Local Journal. Three prizes are offered - 1st £5, 2nd £3, and 3rd £2.

(f) On Saturday, the 6th June, 1953, the Carnival Committee have arranged to have their Annual Carnival to be followed by a Carnival Ball in the evening, at the Mechanics Institute, Horwich.

Coronation Party for the Coronation of Queen Elizabeth II in June 1953. The party was held in Brownlow Road.

St. Mary's Church Sermons. Circa 1925.

Anderton Waterfall. 1944. Children cool off in the waters of the River Douglas during the Second World War.

Horwich Parish Church processions during the late 1940's.

Horwich Co-op Hall Singing Guild. 1933.

Horwich Amateur Operatic Society at the Mechanics' Institute,
Chorley New Road, Horwich. 1960.

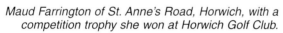

Maud Farrington of St. Anne's Road, Horwich, with a
competition trophy she won at Horwich Golf Club.

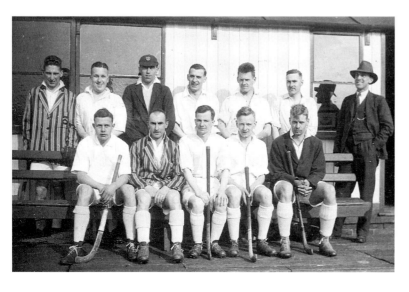

L.M.S. Hockey Team, Horwich Locomotive Works.
Circa 1930.

L.M.S. Ladies Hockey Team. Circa 1935.

Members of the Hurst family enjoy a tennis match on the R.M.I. Recreation Ground. Circa 1900.

Horwich Athletic A.F.C. 1909/1910, taken in Lever Park, Rivington.

Horwich Celtic F.C. Circa 1930.

WITH SATCHEL AND SHINING MORNING FACE

Until early this century the system of education in this country was extremely complicated. Elementary education was largely in the hands of school boards which received Government grants and rate aid, whilst voluntary bodies who undertook the provision of elementary education received grants but no rate aid. A number of school boards were also providing secondary education, and technical education had been put into the hands of the newly formed county and county borough councils who were empowered to levy a rate for this purpose.

A Royal Commission on Secondary Education was appointed in 1894 with the terms of reference, "to consider what are the best methods of establishing a well-organised system of Secondary Education in England taking into account existing deficiencies and having regard to such local sources of revenue from endowment or otherwise as are available or may be made available for this purpose, and to make recommendations accordingly". The Commission, under the chairmanship of James Bryce, reported in 1895 and recommended as follows:- There should be a unified Central Authority for education, presided over by a Minister responsible to Parliament. Its function would be to supervise the Secondary Education of the country and to bring about a harmony and a co-operation among the various agencies which had been found wanting. The report also advocated that in every county and county borough there should be set up a local authority for all types of secondary education.

The Bryce Commission report contains the basis for much of the educational progress that has been made in this country since the beginning of the twentieth century. It was enacted into law on the 20th December 1902, following the Boer War, having been sponsored by the Prime Minister, A.J. Balfour. The provisions of the Bill set up 120 Local Education Authorities throughout England and Wales, thus introducing a co-ordinated national system of education.

Robert Morant was appointed to the post of Permanent Secretary to the newly formed Board of Education and, among many pioneering initiatives, issued a series of regulations concerning elementary and secondary schools; and the training of pupil-teachers. He was responsible for the new official policy towards elementary education which was, briefly, "to form and strengthen the character and to develop the intelligence of children entrusted to it, and to make the best use of the school years available, in assisting both boys and girls, according to their different needs, to fit themselves, practically as well as intellectually, for the work of life". Morant received a knighthood for his services to Education in 1907.

There are many schools in Horwich which cater for the needs of both children and mature students and a cross selection of photographs is included to record some of the happiest days of life.

Lord Street Primary School, Horwich. May Day 1938.

THE OLD SCHOOL, HORWICH,
Near BOLTON.

H. M. INSPECTORS' REPORTS.

Mr. JOHN EVANS appears to have an excellent mode of imparting instruction to his Boys, and impressing it on their memories. His School also does him great credit.

This School is progressing well. The instruction appears much improved and the order is good.

The order in this School is very good. The instruction is progressing fairly. The Writing is especially well taught.

The instruction in this School has improved. The order is very good, and the general tone of the School satisfactory.

This School is in good order, and the instruction does credit to Mr. EVANS.

This School is going on well, and the children's knowledge is very creditable.

The attainments here continue very satisfactory.

Mr. EVANS produces good results and maintains order well. The Reading is fluent and creditable. The exercises in Arithmetic were quickly and accurately done.

This School is in good order and well taught.

The order and teaching are very creditable.

The order is good. The instruction generally fair throughout and of a creditable character.

THE SUBJECTS TAUGHT ARE:

Reading, Writing, Arithmetic, Grammar, Geography, Vocal Music, and Freehand Drawing in connection with the Science and Art Department, London.

FREE-HAND DRAWING.

At the Examination, held in March, 1875, the undermentioned obtained certificates; the first two being marked excellent were also awarded prizes by the Department:—JAMES KAY JOLLY, THOMAS PASS, JAMES HART, ALFRED CHIPPENDALE, WILLIAM LONGWORTH, and WILLIAM MARSDEN. Thirty-two others gave satisfactory evidence of having been taught Drawing.

RELIGIOUS INSTRUCTION.—The School opens and closes with prayer, and a portion of Scripture is read to the Scholars daily by the Master, with simple comments inculcating those christian virtues and moral principles which, ostensibly, are the characteristics and acknowledged guides of all sects and all parties.

Under the will of the late Joseph Ridgway, Esq., READING and WRITING are taught to forty poor children free. These are selected from those most regular and punctual in their attendance at School, and for the extra subjects included in the curriculum of the School, and for expenses of reading-books, pens, ink, fuel, &c., the small charge of one penny each per week is made.

BOYS ADMITTED FROM SIX YEARS OF AGE.

FEES:—Lowest class and under seven years of age, 3d. per week; over seven, 4d. per week.

Her Majesty's Inspectors' Report for Horwich Parish Church School. 1875.

Class of pupils at Horwich Parish Church School. Circa 1910.

Classroom at Horwich Parish Church School. Circa 1910.

Lord Street Primary School, Horwich. Circa 1910.

Victoria Road, Horwich. Circa 1960. The gabled building on the right is the Holy Family R.C. Primary School, with Horwich College of Further Education on the left.

Lord Street Primary School, Horwich. Circa 1940.

Horwich Holy Family School Group. 1959.

Pupils at Lord Street Primary School being taught the essence of road safety. Circa 1938.

Horwich Parish Church Old Boys' School. Circa 1918.

Pupils at Lord Street Primary School collecting for the troops. 1943.

St. Mary's R.C. School is the building on the right with the cupola. 1919.

Top St. Mary's R.C. Primary School, Chorley New Road, Horwich. 1990's.

Middle: Horwich Senior School, Girls Division. Circa 1950. Miss Green, the head teacher, is on the extreme left.

Bottom: Horwich Senior (County Secondary) School. Circa 1950. This photograph shows the Boys' Division of the school. The head teacher, Mr. Whitehead, is to the left.

Horwich Board School, Scholarship Class. 1927.

Horwich Schools Music Festival. 1948.

Lord Street Primary School. 1990.

Stock's Park School, Horwich. 1994.

Chorley New Road Council (Infants) School, Horwich. Circa 1910.

Chorley New Road County Primary School comprises buildings situated on opposite sides of the road. 1994.

Chorley New Road County Primary School, Horwich. 1994. The premises shown in previous photograph face this building. The junction near the pedestrian lights is Victoria Road.

Horwich Senior School Choir. Circa 1940.

St. Joseph's R.C. Comprehensive, Chorley New Road, Horwich. 1994.

St. Catherine's School, Horwich. February, 1936.

Lee Lane Congregational School, Horwich. Circa 1985.

St. Catherine's C of E School, Horwich. Circa 1920.

HEALTH AND WELFARE

FALL BIRCH HOSPITAL, LOSTOCK.

FALL BIRCH HOSPITAL, LOSTOCK.

The foundation stone laying ceremony for Fall Birch Hospital took place on the 23rd April 1903, and it was formally opened on the 9th March 1905. It was originally used for the treatment of such diseases as typhoid, scarlet fever and tuberculosis. With the gradual eradication of these killer diseases the use for the hospital declined and it eventually housed geriatric patients.

Doctor Bennett, Chairman of Horwich Local Authority, during a civic procession. Circa 1960.

Newspaper report on the opening of Horwich Welfare Clinic, Jones Street, Horwich.

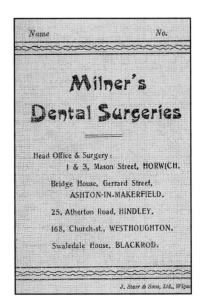

Appointment card for Mrs. Code, 123 Chorley New Road, Horwich, for dental treatment.

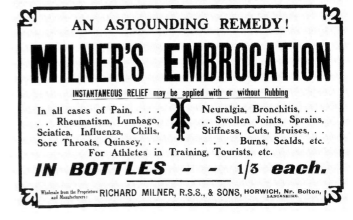

Horwich St. John Ambulance Brigade members. Circa 1950.

BLACKSMITHS

At a time when horse transport was the chief means of travel there were several blacksmiths operating in the Horwich area including R & J Fairclough of The Forge, Emmett Street, Milner's Smithy and the well known Bob's Smithy on the boundary with Bolton.

The Forge, Emmett Street, Horwich, operated by the Fairclough family. Circa 1880.

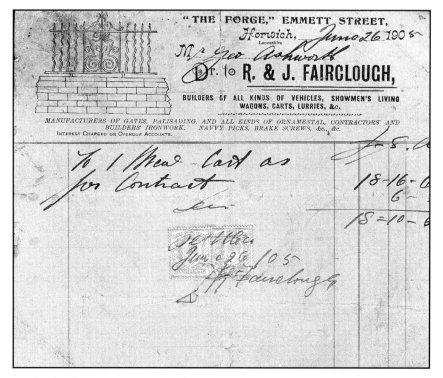

Invoice for the construction of a new cart, supplied to George Ashworth of Rivington, dated 26th June 1905.

Milner's Bridgefoot Smithy, Horwich. 1910. Mr. Milner is standing on the extreme right, whilst his two sons shoe the horse.

Mr. Owen of Owen's Farm, Horwich, photographed outside Mill Hole Cottage. Circa 1920.

Horwich Central Club outing. 1901.

Chorley Old Road showing Bob's Smithy. Circa 1920. The tall chimney can be seen to the right of the picture adjoining two other properties. The Bob's Smithy pub is the whitewashed building at the Bolton end of the terrace on the left.

Livesey's wagonette outside Lee Lane Congregational Chapel. 1920.

Church Street, Horwich. Circa 1920. An excellent view of Church Street, from the Horwich Picture Palace looking past the Bridge Hotel towards the Victoria Wesleyan Chapel on Victoria Road. The postcard was published by H. Fletcher, Stationer of Horwich.

VETERINARY SURGEONS

Much of Horwich was given over to agricultural land and just as important in their own way as the blacksmiths were the veterinary surgeons who tended the animals.

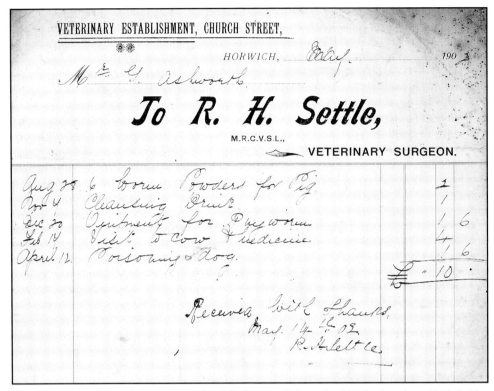

Invoice for 10 shillings (50 new pence) to Mr. George Ashworth of Rivington, from R.H. Settle, Veterinary Surgeon of Church Street, for treatment to animals. The account was settled on the 14th May 1902.

Anyon Kay who had a butchery business on Lee Lane, Horwich, riding near to Wallsuches. Circa 1900.

HORWICH TRAMS

Prior to 1879 Messrs Edmund Holden and Company of Clarence Yard, Bradshawgate, Bolton, operated horse-drawn buses on routes in and around Bolton. One of their routes was from the Victoria Tram Terminus in Bolton to Horwich. An old barn, which once stood near to the junction of Chorley New Road and Ox Hey Lane, was used as a stable and fodder store for the horses.

Whilst private enterprise had been largely responsible for establishing a transport system in the area the various constituent local authorities viewed the provision of public transport as an undertaking which was essentially their responsibility. In the 1870's Bolton Corporation along with the local Boards for Astley Bridge and Farnworth promoted the 'Bolton and Suburban Tramways Order' which was enacted in 1878. This statute authorised the construction of tram track in the district on which horse-drawn trams could be operated. The cost of such construction was £4,000 per mile and between 1880 and 1893 a total of 18 track miles was laid. Messrs Holden & Co., became lessees of the tramway route in 1880 and from this date took out a number of leases. All the leases were eventually scheduled for expiry in 1903.

Bolton Corporation became increasingly keen to take over the tram service in its entirety because it was a good revenue producer and with a view to improving the system examined several steam tram engines, cable tramways and ammonia gas drive cars. In the event electrically powered trams became a favoured option. A decision was taken to build an electricity generating station to provide the motive power for the tramway system and this was constructed in Spa Road, Bolton, and opened in 1894. Three years later, in 1897, Bolton Corporation received powers to operate the entire tram system within and adjacent to the Borough of Bolton and to, and within the Urban District of Horwich.

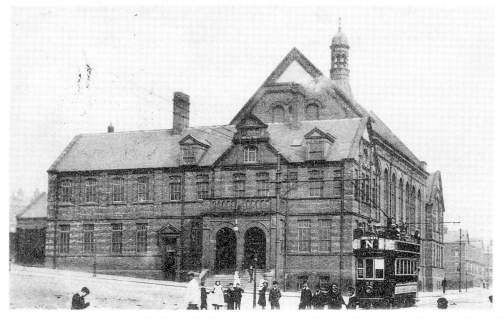

Open topped tram outside the Railway Mechanics' Institute on Chorley New Road, Horwich. Circa 1905.

The position of Messrs Holden & Co., became less tenable and in June 1899 the company sold out their various leases to Bolton Corporation along with their operating stock which included 48 trams and 350 horses. The price negotiated for the sell out was £58,000. Technically, Holden's lease was scheduled to expire in 1903 but this was in fact nullified when the company sold out to Bolton Corporation. Nevertheless, it was necessary to obtain sanction from the Board of Trade to commence the introduction of electric powered trams from the 8th December 1899. The actual date set for Bolton Corporation to take over the running of the system was the 1st January 1900.

On the 2nd January 1900, the day following the take-over, the last horse-drawn tram was operated. Electrically powered trams ran from Bolton to Lostock along Chorley New Road and on the 13th April 1900 the service was extended to run as far as the Crown Hotel at Horwich. A tram depot was built on Chorley New Road, Horwich, during 1900 and remained in service until the closure of the service to Horwich on the 7th October 1946. A loop line which junctioned with the tramway along Chorley New Road, Horwich, and ran along Victoria Road and Lee Lane to the Crown Hotel was opened on the 19th May 1900. The line was however relatively short lived being abandoned in December 1907.

The 122 bus service between Bolton and Horwich via Chorley Old Road commenced on the 16th August 1926 and following the demise of the tram all services were operated by motor buses. The last tram ran in Bolton on the 30th March 1947 signalling the end of an era.

Horwich Tram Shed, Chorley New Road, Horwich. Circa 1940. The depot was built during 1900 and the words 'BOLTON CORPORATION CAR SHED' can be seen in the stonework above the large opening. Horwich Spiritualist Church is the single storey building next to the depot.

Lee Lane, Horwich. Circa 1905. The single tramway is visible in the cobbled roadway. Mason Memorial Chapel is on the right.

An excellent view along Chorley New Road, Horwich, from the Black Dog public house, which is on the extreme right. A double tram track ran the length of Chorley New Road.

Boarding a tram outside the Black Dog. Circa 1910.

Horwich Crown Hotel was the terminus for the service.

The harsh winter of 1940 caused severe problems for the transport services. The scene shows snow clearing on the railway bridge in Chorley New Road, Horwich.

Church Street was a difficult climb for the trams particularly during ice and snow. A tram pole can be seen outside the low building on the right, which is Bridgefoot Smithy. The Bridge Hotel is next, then the Conservative Club, with the Victoria Wesleyan Chapel far left. Circa 1910.

(Above) The Crown Terminus from Crown Lane. 1935.

Lee Lane, Horwich. Circa 1905. The tram track and overhead power lines are visible on this photograph. Lee Lane Post Office can be seen on the left.

ADAM MASON & SONS

Adam Mason was born in 1822, the son of Thomas Mason, a staunch non-conformist, who had a grocery shop in Church Street, Horwich, established prior to 1800. Adam had a brother Thomas and a sister Rachel. The two sons carried on the family business on the death of their father. Adam, however, had other business interests and commenced a brick and tile works at Montcliffe, where coal was also mined. He married a Miss Evans of Preston and built a matrimonial home at Montcliffe. The couple had two sons; Herbert E. Mason and W. E. Mason; who were taken into the family business which then traded as 'Adam Mason & Sons'. A sanitary pipe works was established in Chorley New Road, Horwich and the works of Mr. Andrew Peak were eventually absorbed into the business. His wife died about 1880, and following his retirement in 1890, Adam Mason went to live at Southport accompanied by his sister, Rachel. He died on Monday, 1st October 1900, in Southport.

For over 50 years he gave service to New Chapel where, up to the time of his death, he officiated as an honorary deacon. He was one of the first members of Horwich Liberal Club and held various public offices locally including superintendent of New Chapel Sunday School, treasurer of the sick society and a trustee of the Congregational Chapel.

In the Post Office Directory for Horwich, for 1890 / 91, Adam Mason and Sons, are described as "colliery proprietors, Montcliffe Colliery, and manufacturers, of Bessemer tuyeres, fire-bricks & tiles, Pearl Brook Fire Clay Works."

Tuyeres, incidentally, is from the French meaning 'blast-pipe'. Tuyeres were used in the manufacture of Bessemer steel. They were made from fire clay and were round varying in diameter from 3 to 7 inches, and in length from 12 to 24 inches. The tuyeres were perforated along their whole length. A blast-pipe was attached to the lower end of the tuyeres and when molten iron was poured over them in a 'converter', air was blasted through the tuyeres. The result being the production of Bessemer steel.

OFFICES AND SHOWROOMS:
PEARL BROOK WORKS, HORWICH.

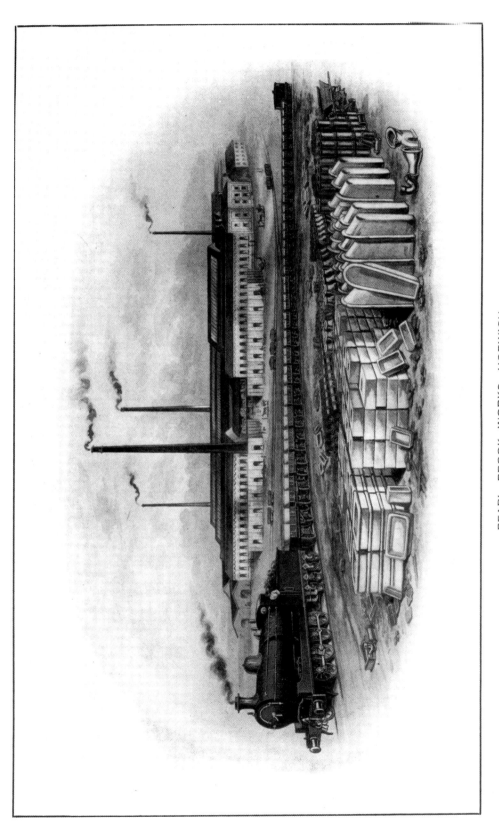

PEARL BROOK WORKS, HORWICH

JOHN CRANKSHAW CO., LTD

On Saturday, 19th March 1898, the company of John Crankshaw Limited, was registered with a capital of £20,000 in £1 shares, to acquire certain lands, brickworks and buildings at Horwich; and to carry on the business of builders' contractors, builders' merchants, etc. This firm took over the business of Adam Mason & Sons.

John Crankshaw Co., Ltd, manufactured a wide range of salt glazed stoneware, including pipes from 3" to 36" in diameter, drainage fittings, chimney pots, aerating tiles, firebricks and tiles, electric cable conduits, garden vases and tiles, cattle troughs, latrine ranges, etc. In addition, a range of metal products were produced such as cast-iron manhole and inspection chamber covers, gully grates and step irons. The trademark used was a "STONITE".

THE JOHN CRANKSHAW CO.'S WORKS. HORWICH.

ANOTHER VIEW OF THE JOHN CRANKSHAW CO.'S WORKS. HORWICH.

A SAMPLE OF JOHN CRANKSHAW & CO'S PRODUCTS FROM THEIR 1917 CATALOGUE.

ENAMELLED FIRECLAY LAVATORIES.

FIG. 713.
15½″ × 35½″

FIG. 714.
14″ × 37″

CHIMNEY POTS (BUFF OR SALT GLAZED)

GARDEN VASES.

FIG. 752.
3′ 6″ high.

FIG. 751.
3′ 0″ high

FIG. 753.
3′ 6″ high.

One of John Crankshaw's Wagons. Circa 1930.

PEARL BROOK FIRE CLAY WORKS AND MONTCLIFFE COLLIERY.

BESSEMER TUYERES &c

TELEGRAMS-
MASON-HORWICH.

Horwich Sep. 13 1890

Nª BOLTON.

Dear Mr Crowther,

Allow me very heartily
to congratulate you upon
your marriage. I sincerely
trust that you and your
dear wife may together have
a long, happy, and useful
life. Much of this I expect
will depend upon your own
two selves. That God may may
abundantly bless you is

my most sincere wish.
I am glad you have had
such fine weather, and I
trust I may be so fortunate
in this respect when my
time comes to do the same
thing as you today

Yours Very faithfully

J. Morgan

W. R. PICKUP & CO, LTD

W. R. Pickup & Co., Ltd, traded from Pearl Brook Works, Horwich and are described as manufacturers of porcelain, enamelled fireclay baths, lavatories, urinals, sinks, closets, &c.

Correspondence (reproduced) between R. M. Cameron, Estate Officer for the Liverpool Corporation Waterworks and W. R. Pickup, suggest that both Crankshaw's and Pickup's worked in conjunction. In addition, the 1917 trades catalogue issued by John Crankshaw, Pearl Brook Works, Horwich, contains a print of their offices and showrooms which traded under the name of W. R. Pickup & Co., Ltd. Pickup's was in fact a subsidiary of Crankshaws early this century. The two concerns were eventually amalgamated when the Associated Clay Industries Ltd., took over the works sometime prior to 1948.

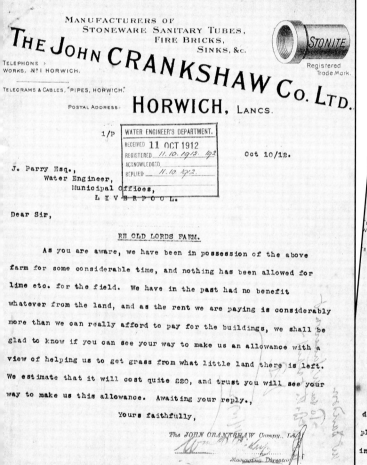

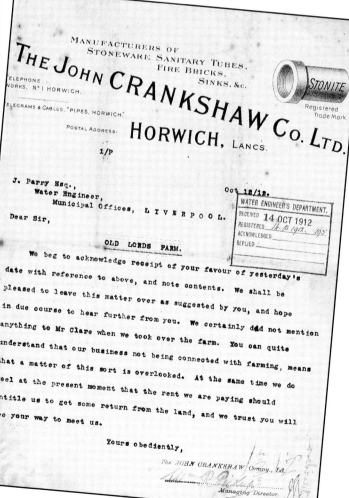

W. R. PICKUP'S CHEMICAL WORKS, HORWICH

Pickup's Chemical Works, Horwich. Circa 1890. The works were situated near the junction of Chorley New Road and Mason Street.

BRICK MAKING

In addition to John Crankshaw Co., Ltd, there were several brickmakers who operated in Horwich, including A. E. Yates & Co., Crown Brickworks, Chorley New Road; William Fletcher & Sons of Brookfield Works; Andrew Peak of Wilderswood Fireclay Works, Chorley New Road; and William Dougill and Sons of Mount Pleasant Machine-Made Plastic Brick and Terra Cotta Works, Chorley New Road.

On Saturday, 19th February 1849, an advertisement appeared in the Bolton Chronicle relating to 'Five Houses Fire Brick and Tile Works' on Horwich Moor, which read as follows: -

'TO BE LET - An extensive and well established Fire Brick and Tile Works, situated at the Five Houses, Horwich Moor, the present proprietor being desirous of retiring from the business.

The works are complete with Steam Engine, Grinding and Crushing apparatus, Stoves, Drying Houses, Ovens, Moulds and every convenience for carrying out business.

The clay and coal being of superior quality, and are got on the premises at very trifle expense.

P.S. Any person taking the works can be accommodated with five or six acres of land and a few cottages adjoining.

For particulars apply to Mr. Wm. Garbutt in the premises, or on Monday at the King's Arms and Four Horse Shoes, Bolton.

Andrew Peak, brick and tile manufacturer of Horwich.

CROWN BRICK WORKS, HORWICH. (Result of a thunderstorm) 25.5.09.

Crown Hotel, Horwich. 1900. The ornate lamp was erected in 1876 by the generosity of Andrew Peak.

COPY OF INDENTURE RELATING TO LAND IN HORWICH PURCHASED BY ANDREW PEAK IN 1884.

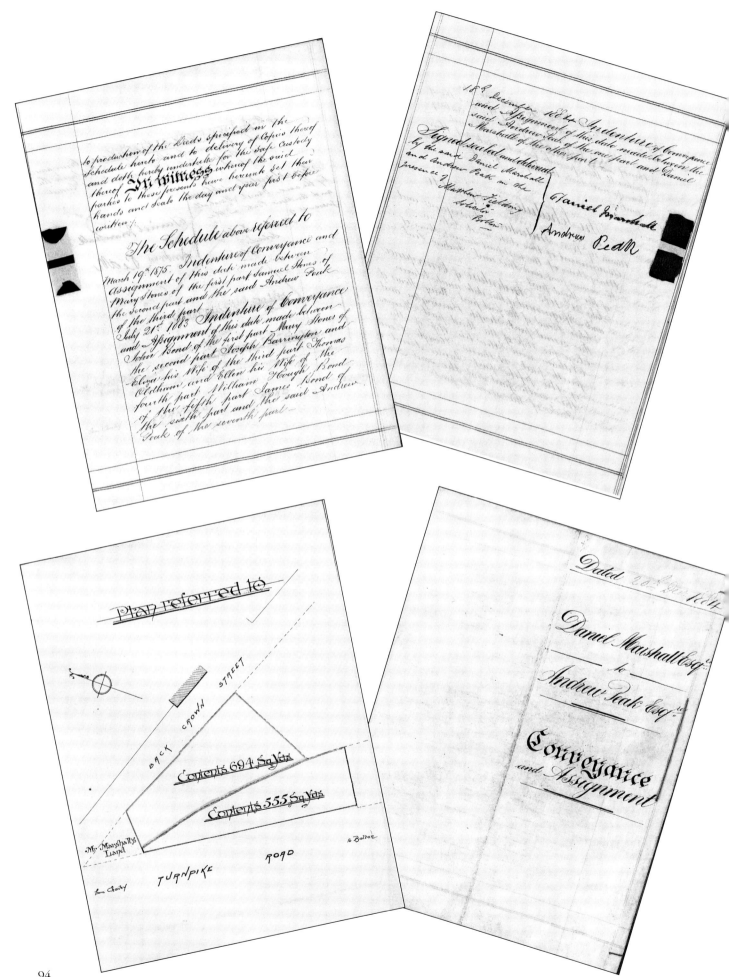

to production of the Deeds specified in the
Schedule hereto and to delivery of Copies thereof
and doth hereby undertake for the safe Custody
thereof whereof the said
parties to these presents have hereunto set their
hands and seals the day and year first before
written.

In Witness

The Schedule above referred to

March 19th 1875. Indenture of Conveyance and
Assignment of this date made between
Mary Stones of the first part Samuel Stones of
the second part and the said Andrew Peak
of the third part

July 21st 1883 Indenture of Conveyance
and Assignment of this date made between
Mary Stones of
John Bond of the first part Mary Stones of
the second part Joseph Barrington and
Eliza his Wife of the third part Thomas
Oldham and Ellen his Wife of the
fourth part William Hough Bond
of the fifth part James Bond of
the sixth part and the said Andrew
Peak of the seventh part—

18th December 1884 Indenture of Conveyance
and Assignment of this date made between the
said Andrew Peak of the one part and Daniel
Marshall of the other part

Signed, sealed and delivered
by the said Daniel Marshall
and Andrew Peak in the
presence of
Matthew Fielding
Solicitor
Bolton

Daniel Marshall

Andrew Peak

Plan referred to

BACK CROWN STREET

Contents 694 Sq Yds

Contents 555 Sq Yds

Mr. Marshall's Land

from Chorley   TURNPIKE ROAD   to Bolton

Dated 20th Dec 1884

Daniel Marshall Esqre

to

Andrew Peak Esqre

Conveyance
and Assignment

COOKE & NUTTALL LTD.

Cooke & Nuttall Ltd, Vale Paper Mills, Horwich, was founded in 1862 by Mr. Leonard Cooke and on his death was carried on by his son, Horace Cooke. Initially, the firm was involved in producing Wrapping and Duplex Papers dealing with about 20 to 30 tons per week. One machine (a Fourdrinier) was then in use.

In 1898 Mr. T. Y. Nuttall, late of the Darwen Paper Company, joined forces with Mr. Cooke and introduced fresh capital. The mills at Horwich were totally rebuilt during 1898 and completely re-equipped throughout with modern high-speed machinery. New engines and boilers were installed and a new wide paper machine erected. Cooke & Nuttall Ltd, then became the trade name for the organisation.

In 1920 Mr. W. E. Nuttall, son of Mr. T. Y. Nuttall one of the founding fathers, joined the Board of Directors. Mr. Horace Cooke retired in 1917, and in July 1920, Mr. T. Y. Nuttall died.

It was the policy of the Directors to make against orders received and such was the demand for the firm's product that output rose steadily. For many years the company specialised in Kraft paper and thairs was the first mill in Great Britain to take up its production seriously.

View of Mills.

Mr. Horace Cooke son of the founder of Cooke & Nuttall Ltd.

Mr. T. Y. Nuttall who co-founded Cooke & Nuttall Ltd., in 1898.

Aerial view of Mills.

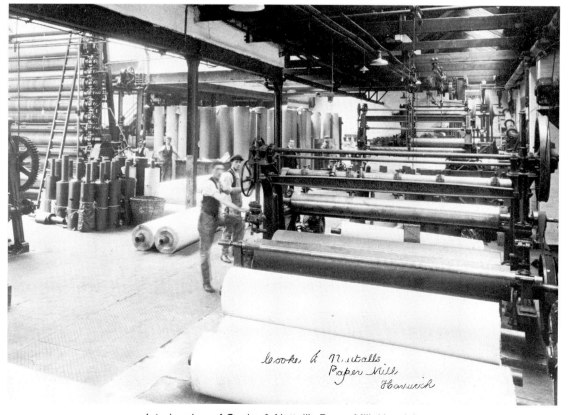

Interior view of Cooke & Nuttall's Paper Mill, Horwich.

Production line at Cooke and Nuttall's Paper Mill.

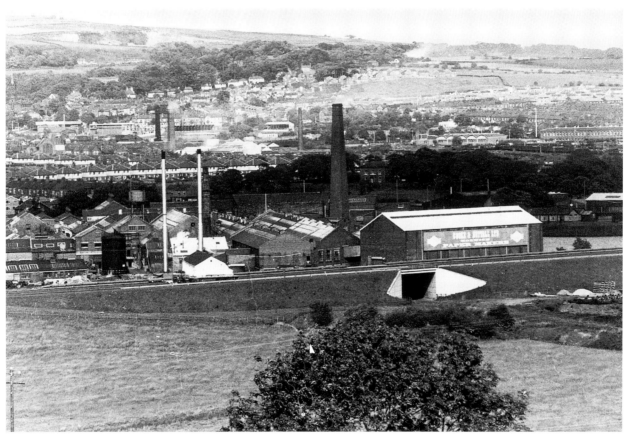

Cooke and Nuttall's Paper Mill from the M.61 Motorway. Circa 1960. (Photo. David Gibbons)

W.T.TAYLOR'S TEXTILE MILL

Aerial view of Horwich 1988. (Bolton Evening News Photograph) The view covers an area roughly between Victoria Road on the left to Ainsworth Avenue on the right, along Chorley New Road. The mill at the bottom left CHORTEX STOTT & SMITH GROUP LTD (WAVECREST)' was originally opened in 1904 as W. T. Taylor.

W.R. Taylor's portrait hangs on the wall of the boardroom at Victoria Mills and standing second from left and on the far right are the founder's two sons.

Office staff party at W. R. Taylor's Victoria Mill. Circa 1955.

Workers inside Victoria Mills, Horwich.
Circa 1960.

Results of a fire in the Dye House at
Victoria Mills, Horwich.

Extensive damage caused by fire in the
Dye House at Victoria Mills, Horwich.

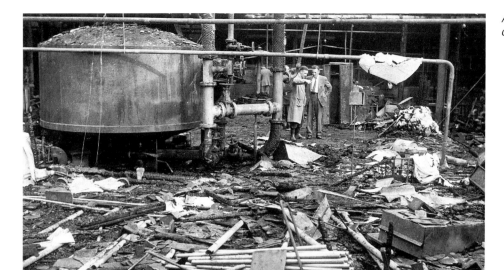

Another view of the devastation caused.

Clean-up operations at Victoria Mills following the devastating fire.

Essential damping down operations following a fire at textile premises exacerbates the scale of the damage caused and increases the work of clearance.

WILDERSWOOD MILL, HORWICH

Wilderswood Mill, Horwich. Circa 1895. Mill Hole cottage is the whitewashed property (centre right) with Factory Hill Cottages standing directly behind. The Mill is left of centre with Wilderswood House and stables far left. William Bennett who owned the mill founded Horwich Races with Richard Brownlow and Mr. Munday of Preston. Wilderswood Mill was demolished in 1911 and Factory Hill Cottages in 1939.

Wilderswood Mill. Circa 1900.

This postcard view of Wilderswood issued around 1900 is wrongly entitled Tiger's Clough, Horwich.
Wilderswood Mill and Mill Hole Cottage can be seen.

Luke Berry of Chorley published this view of Tiger's Clough on the Rivington / Horwich boundary. Circa 1900.

BLEACHING AND FINISHING

John Longworth (of Horwich) Ltd., had a bleaching and finishing works in Bridge Street, Horwich and the photograph included below are of the workforce. Alfred J. Ingham is recorded as the manager of the works in the 1932 copy of Tillotsons Bolton Directory.

Longworth's Bleachworks Staff, Horwich. Circa 1910. Pauline Hudson and Sidney Lomax have been identified amongst the group.

Wallsuches House, which is situated in the grounds of Wallsuches Bleachworks. Circa 1900.

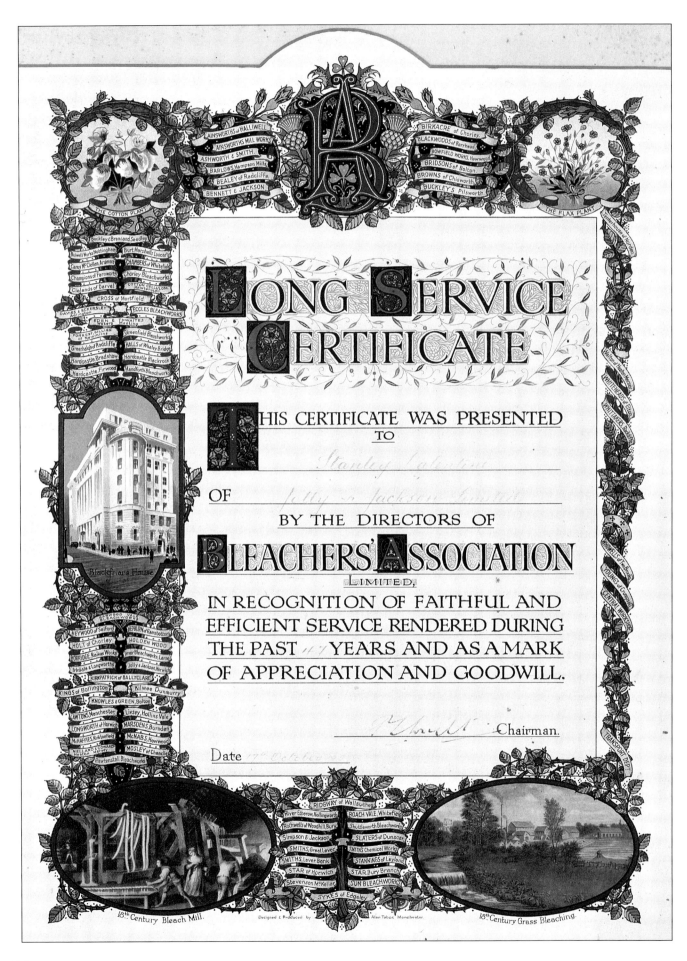

LONG SERVICE CERTIFICATE

THIS CERTIFICATE WAS PRESENTED
TO

Stanley Valentine

OF *Jolly & Jackson Limited*

BY THE DIRECTORS OF

BLEACHERS' ASSOCIATION
LIMITED,

IN RECOGNITION OF FAITHFUL AND
EFFICIENT SERVICE RENDERED DURING
THE PAST YEARS AND AS A MARK
OF APPRECIATION AND GOODWILL.

_____ Chairman.

Date _____

THE COTTON PLANT

THE FLAX PLANT

AINSWORTHS of HALLIWELL
AINSWORTHS MILL WORKS
ASHWORTH & SMITH
BARLOWS Hampson Mills
BEALEY of Radcliffe
BENNETT & JACKSON

BIRKACRE of Chorley
BLACKWOODS of Barrhead
BOWFIELD WORKS, Howwood
BRIDSONS of Bolton
BROWNS of Chisworth
BUCKLEY'S Pilsworth

Buckley & Brennand Seedley
Bulwell Works Nottingham
Carey McClellen Ardmore
Champions of Farnworth
Cleilands of Darvel
CROSS of Mortfield
DAVIES & ECKERSLEY Adlington
EDEN & THWAITES Keighley
FORREST GILLIES of Newmilns
Greenhalgh of Radcliffe
Hardcastle Bradshaw
Hardcastle Firwood

Burt Marshalls Lunearty
CHAMBERS of Whitefield
Chorley Bleachworks
COTTON CELLULOSE
ECCLES BLEACHWORKS
Greenfield Bleachworks
HALLS of Whaley Bridge
Hardcastle Blackrock
Handforth Bleachworks

Blackfriars House

HEYWOOD of Salford
HOLT of Chorley
HORRIDGE, Railway Works
Irkdale & Longworths
KIRKPATRICK of BALLYCLARE
KINGS of Bollington
KNOWLES & GREEN, Bolton
LAWTONS, Manchester
LONGWORTH of Horwich
McHAFFIES, Kirk tonfield
MELLAND & COWARD Heaton
Rawtenstall Bleachworks

HEPBURN of Ramsbottom
HOLDEN WOOD
Inver Bleachworks, Larne
Jolly & Jackson Norwich
Kilwee Dunmurry
Livsey, Hollins Vale
MARSDENS, Burnden
McNAB'S, Howwood
MOSLEY of Cheadle

RIDGWAY of Wallsuches
River Etherow, Hollingworth
Rothwells of Woodhill, Bury
Simpson & Jackson
SMITHS, Great Lever
SMITHS, Lever Bank
STAR of Horwich
Stevenson McKellar
SYKES of Edgeley

ROACH VALE, Whitefield
Shuttleworth Bleachworks
SLATERS of Dunscar
SMITHS Chemical Works
STANNINGS of Leyland
STAR, Bury Branch
SUN BLEACHWORKS

18th Century Bleach Mill.

Designed & Produced by Alan Tabor, Manchester.

18th Century Grass Bleaching.

106

HORWICH LOCOMOTIVE WORKS

Horwich Locomotive Works existed in the town from the mid 1880's until 1983 and played an immense part in the history of the surrounding area. It would be remiss of me not to mention the works although it is the subject of a dedicated history entitled 'Horwich Locomotive Works' which was published in 1996.

Aerial view of Horwich Locomotive Works. 1930.

British Rail Staff outside the works, with the Works Manager G.F.S. Staley. 1974.

Horwich Locomotive Works staff outside the main office building. Circa 1950.

Staff inside the Drawing Office at Horwich Works. Circa 1950.

Staff photograph taken inside the work's yard. Circa 1950.

MUSIC, SINGING AND DANCING THROUGH THE YEARS

Horwich people have always had the capacity to enjoy themselves. Those people who work hard generally play hard and there is much ephemeral evidence of activities down the years. The Mechanics' Institute and the Co-operative Hall were among the more popular venues for staging dances. A selection of material is included to illustrate this aspect of community life.

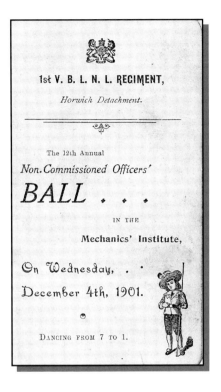

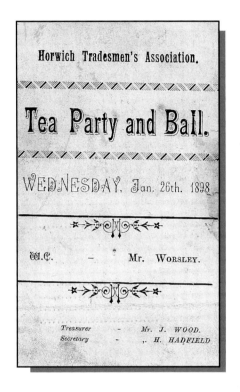

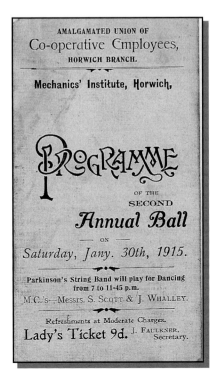

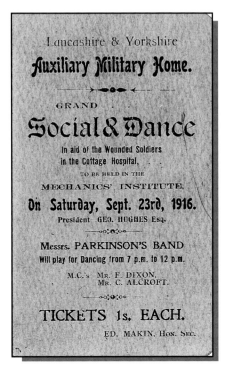

Horwich Railway Mechanics' Institute from a post card, postally used on the 23rd July 1952.

Horwich Schools Music Festival 1948. The venue for this festival was the Methodist Sunday School on Victoria Road, Horwich.

Horwich Music Festival held at Victoria Road Wesleyan School. 1959.

*Andrea Smith (nee Mason) of Adlington, Winner of the Horwich Musical
Festival Rose Bowl. 1981*

Horwich Industrial Co-operative Society staff outside the Central Hall on Lee Lane. Circa 1930.
The upper storey of these premises was used for dances, etc.

Victoria Methodist Sunday School, Victoria Road, Horwich. Circa 1910.

Horwich Coronets Dance Troupe. Circa 1955.

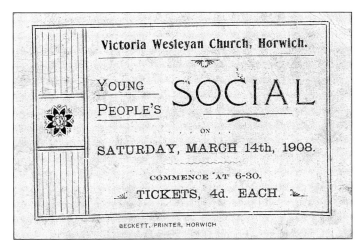

Victoria Wesleyan Church, Horwich.

YOUNG
PEOPLE'S **SOCIAL**

.. ON ..

SATURDAY, MARCH 14th, 1908.

COMMENCE AT 6-30.

TICKETS, 4d. EACH.

BECKETT, PRINTER, HORWICH.

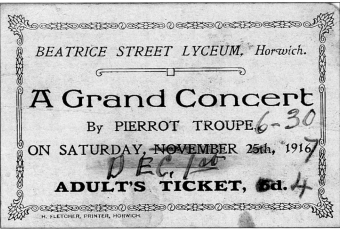

BEATRICE STREET LYCEUM, Horwich.

A Grand Concert

By PIERROT TROUPE. 6-30

ON SATURDAY, NOVEMBER 25th, 1916

DEC. 1st

ADULT'S TICKET, 5d. 4

H. FLETCHER, PRINTER, HORWICH.

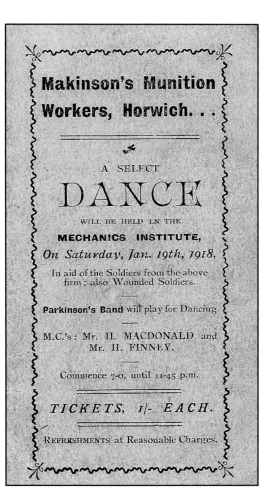

Makinson's Munition Workers, Horwich. . .

A SELECT

DANCE

WILL BE HELD IN THE

MECHANICS INSTITUTE,

On Saturday, Jan. 19th, 1918,

In aid of the Soldiers from the above firm ; also Wounded Soldiers.

Parkinson's Band will play for Dancing

M.C.'s : Mr. H. MACDONALD and Mr. H. FINNEY.

Commence 7-0, until 11-45 p.m.

TICKETS, 1/- EACH.

REFRESHMENTS at Reasonable Charges.

Horwich Carnival procession along Chorley New Road, Horwich. Circa 1930. On the left of this group of black and white minstrels is Arthur Hudson.

BRASS ENSEMBLE

Horwich Lancashire & Yorkshire Locomotive Prize Band. Circa 1910.

Horwich Band. Circa 1930.

Horwich Public Prize Band. Circa 1925.

TURNPIKES

CHORLEY OLD ROAD

The Bolton and Nightingales' Trust turnpiked Chorley Old Road (B. 6226) in 1763. Nightingales, from which the name of the trust is derived, was a house in Heath Charnock; once occupied by Viscount Cardwell of Ellerbeck who entered Parliament as a 'Peelite' in 1842 and was Secretary for War in Gladstone's Government. Despite owning Ellerbeck Hall, Viscount Cardwell only used the Nightingales, a property on the estate, as an occasional residence. There was a toll-gate situated near to the junction of Crown Lane and Scholes Bank, Horwich. The title of the Toll Bar Inn which presently stands at this junction stems from the period when tolls were payable for use of the road. The Crown Hotel, the Black Bull and the Blundell Arms licensed houses were regularly used by travellers for stabling and accommodation. On the 1st November 1877 the Bolton and Nightingales' Trust ceased to operate. The toll gates at Horwich were actually sold by auction on the 24th October 1877. One of the original gates was owned for many years by Mr. G. Brookes, a funeral director, who lived in Scholes Bank.

SCHOLES BANK

Aerial view of Scholes Bank at the junction with Dryfield Lane. The property belongs to the North West Water Authority and was occupied by their employees. The filter beds can be seen top left.

Scholes Bank, Horwich. Circa 1946. The building on the extreme right was a small bleachworks known locally as 'Tottering Temple'. It was demolished during the road widening scheme for Scholes Bank.

View looking down Scholes Bank, Horwich, from the Crown Hotel. Circa 1910.

LEVER PARK AVENUE

Lever Park Avenue from Scholes Bank. Circa 1920.

The two granite pillars at the entrance to Lever Park Avenue were erected in memory of the first Viscount Leverhulme, who made a gift of Lever Park to the people of Bolton and the surrounding district. The pillars were erected on behalf of his son during 1934.

LEE LANE

Lee Lane, Horwich, viewed from Scholes Bank. Circa 1920.
On the right of the photograph is the Crown Hotel with the Queen's Head Hotel on the left.

Brownlow Road junctions off Lee Lane by the side of the Saddle Inn. Postcard view circa 1950.

LEE LANE / WINTER HEY LANE

Lee Lane and Winter Hey Lane, Horwich, contain much of the commercial and retail property in the town centre and the junction of these two roads was a favourite location for photographers as these early twentieth century views show.

One of the more familiar post card views of Horwich streets is the one shown above which dates from the early years of the twentieth century.

Tram tracks in the centre of Lee Lane date this photograph between 1900 and 1907. It is believed that the police officer on the left is Inspector Ryder of Horwich Police.

WINTER HEY LANE

Winter Hey Lane runs between Lee Lane and Chorley New Road and is a relatively busy thoroughfare. Efforts have been made in recent years to close off access into Winter Hey Lane from Lee Lane but this proved so unpopular with both traders and the public that the experiment was called off. Traffic signals were however erected at the junction in order to improve road safety.

Winter Hey Lane from Lee Lane, Horwich. Circa 1910. The large brick building on the left was once Craven Heifer public house.

Winter Hey Lane, Horwich. Circa 1916. Fletcher's Printers can be seen at the top of the lane in this interesting old view.

Winter Hey Lane, Horwich. Circa 1950.

Winter Hey Lane, Horwich. Circa 1955.

CHURCH STREET

The B.6226 commences as Lee Lane at the Crown and becomes Church Street for a stretch near to the parish church before the name is again changed to Chorley Old Road.

Church Street, Horwich. Circa 1905. The Victoria Wesleyan Chapel is on the right next to Horwich Police Station. Both these properties were built in 1887 following the arrival of the locomotive works. Hamers were the licensees of the Black Bull Hotel at this time who were supplied by John Sumner of Haigh Brewery. Horwich Parish Church tower can be seen behind the pub.

Close up view of the Black Bull Inn and adjacent properties, 1910

Church Street, Horwich. Circa 1910. The parish church wall and railings are on the right with the steps to stone cottages on the left.

CHORLEY OLD ROAD

Chorley Old Road, Horwich. Circa 1910. This early view shows the stocks on the far right near to the entrance to Fleet Street.

Chorley Old Road at the junction with George's Lane, Bottom o'th Moor, Horwich. Circa 1950.

Chorley Old Road, Montserrat, Bolton. Circa 1930.

CHORLEY NEW ROAD

The final period of turnpike extension was carried out between 1821 and 1842. In 1824 the Bolton and Nightingales Trust obtained Parliamentary sanction for the construction of Chorley New Road (A.673) which branched from the old turnpike road at the top of Scholes Bank.

The Crown Hotel, Horwich, at the junction of Chorley New Road (A.673)
and Lee Lane (B.6226). Circa 1950.

Chorley New Road, Horwich. Circa 1910. The date stone on the building extreme right reads 1885 which was just after the arrival of the locomotive works. The premises are in use as a shop at this time but were eventually taken into use as Horwich Labour Club. Curteis Street runs along the side of the shop. At present the premises are in use as a restaurant.

Chorley New Road, Horwich. Circa 1910. Tram tracks running along the roadway help to date this photograph. The tram-shed can be seen in the centre of the picture.

Chorley New Road, Horwich. Circa 1950. In the distance can be seen the bridge carrying the road over the railway lines from Horwich Railway Station.

ROAD SURFACING

One of the most difficult problems in providing roadways is the construction of a durable surface. In the days when horse drawn transport was predominant it was found that granite setts laid on concrete were desirable, particularly on heavily trafficked roads and uphill sections where the horses could gain better purchase.

During the time that tramways were in operation the sett paving proved advantageous. Tram tracks were carried on a bed of concrete and were held to gauge by transverse tie-bars. The company, which operated the tramway, was held responsible for the road surface between the tracks and on each side of them. Sett paving was preferred because whole sections of roadway could be easily replaced.

As the use of motorised transport increased the sett paving proved too uneven and, to some extent, dangerous. A system of spreading tarmac on the sett paving eventually provided one of a number of solutions. The tar from town gas was considered unsuitable for use because of the potential of polluting water supplies. In 1913 when it was proposed to tarmac the road between Chorley and Bolton, both Chorley Rural District Council and the Bleachers' Association objected on the grounds that water supplies would be affected.

CHORLEY NEW ROAD, HORWICH.

Chorley New Road, Horwich. Circa 1930. W.T. Taylor's Victoria Mill is on the left. The two-way tram tracks are flush with the sett paving.

Chorley New Road, Horwich. Circa 1950. Lilywhite, Ltd., of Brighouse, Yorkshire published this post card view which shows the tarmacadamed road surface along Chorley New Road. Ferretti's ice cream parlour is on the extreme left with The Toll Bar Inn the first building on the right.

Lee Lane, Horwich. Major roadworks in progress during the 1980's.

HORWICH FIRE STATION

A custom built fire station was completed for Horwich Fire Brigade in 1939 and their existing engine was replaced in 1940 by the latest Bedford design.

Horwich Fire Station. 1939. The station is sand-bagged in case of an air aid during the 1939 - 1945 World War. The fire engine shown has solid tyres.

During wartime a number of auxiliary fire fighters were employed to assist the regular crews. The engine shown here was the replacement Bedford fire engine taken into use during 1940.

Lily Leech, aged 19 years, who was the secretary to Horwich's Chief Fire Officer can be seen with members of the local brigade during 1940.

Horwich is presently the responsibility of the Greater Manchester Fire Authority. During 1997 the fire station was completely rebuilt. This photograph shows the demolition of the old building.

The fire brigade in action at a serious fire which broke out at Joshua Kershaw's Leather Works during the 1970's.

The new Horwich Fire Station, Chorley New Road, Horwich. 1999.

PHOTOGRAPHERS

Among the best photographers in Horwich was Ralph Close who had a studio at 167, Chorley New Road, Horwich. Following his death Higgins Studios of Horwich purchased the negatives and continued to issue post card prints bearing their name.

Ralph Close's studio was situated in the premises housing the business of J. Cartmell in this 1920's photograph of a procession along Chorley New Road.

Reverse of a Carte de visite portrait photograph supplied by Ralph Close.

A typical Ralph Close postcard, postally used during 1905. The view was taken from the top of Winter Hey Road looking along Lee Lane.

The wedding of James Bromley and Jessie Harrison at Parsonage Nurseries, Brazley, Horwich, is the subject of this excellent 1910 photograph.

THE WHEELS OF COMMERCE

The establishment of Horwich Locomotive Works in the 1880's upgraded Horwich to township status by increasing the population more than threefold to 12,850 persons. Such a dramatic rise in the number of residents required a proportionate expansion of the commercial trade outlets to satisfy the additional demands for goods and services. Thus, many new businesses were established at this time to complement the existing network. Running a shop or a small business was never an easy option, often entailing long unsociable hours. Difficulties were multiplied during the two World Wars when wage earners were away from their families and trade goods were in short supply or not available. In these difficult times there were many traders who chose to help families through harsh circumstances by allowing them to keep their dignity at no little cost to the shopkeeper. In addition, many retailers held public office and were associated with various church organisations. They were also responsible for many generous benefactions to the town.

It is often said that there is no sentiment in business but the shopkeeper is as dependent on his customers as they are on his good offices.

Photographs of shops and the ephemera of trade, including invoices and advertisements, are extremely popular and the following selection relating to Horwich is intended to illustrate this aspect of community life.

The 'XL' Shoe Shop, 36 Lee Lane, Horwich.

Maud Smith is standing at the door of her sweetshop,
50 Church Street, Horwich.
Her mother lived next door at No. 48 and can be seen far left.

Ferretti's Ice Cream Cart. Circa 1910.

The horse drawing Ferretti's ice cream cart has been decked out in the finest livery as if for some special occasion.

Mr. J. Farrel Smethurst's photographic shop on Chorley New Road, Horwich. Circa 1935.

Horwich Industrial Co-operative Society's Golden Jubilee stand in the Mechanics' Institute on Chorley New Road, Horwich. 1912.

The Maypole Dairy Company, Lee Lane, Horwich. Circa 1910.

Horwich Panel Bowling Club, Ladies Day, 1935. The club comprised many of Horwich's shopkeepers and business people. Anyon Kay is standing to the extreme right and the three men, back row left, are the Barker brothers who owned the Squirrel Hotel. The photograph was taken at the bowling green at the hotel.

Samuel J. Rose's pork butchery shop, 54 Lee Lane, Horwich. Circa 1910.

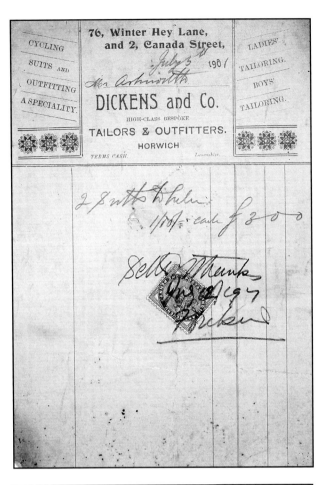

CYCLING
SUITS AND
OUTFITTING
A SPECIALITY.

**76, Winter Hey Lane,
and 2, Canada Street,**

July 3 1901

Mr Ashworth

DICKENS and Co.

HIGH-CLASS BESPOKE

TAILORS & OUTFITTERS.

HORWICH

TERMS CASH.   Lancashire.

LADIES'
TAILORING.
BOYS'
TAILORING.

2 Suits Whilm
1/10/- each £3 0 0

Settd with thanks
Jan 2 1902
Dickens

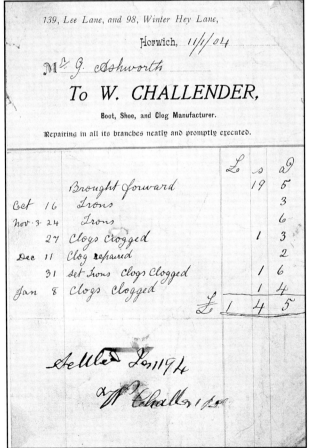

139, Lee Lane, and 98, Winter Hey Lane,

Horwich, 11/1/04

Mr G. Ashworth

To W. CHALLENDER,

Boot, Shoe, and Clog Manufacturer.

Repairing in all its branches neatly and promptly executed.

		£	s	d
	Brought forward		19	5
Oct 16	Irons			3
Nov 3 24	Irons			6
27	Clogs clogged		1	3
Dec 11	Clog repaired			2
31	set Irons clogs clogged		1	6
Jan 8	Clogs clogged		1	4
		£	1 4	5

Settd Jan 11 94
W. Challender

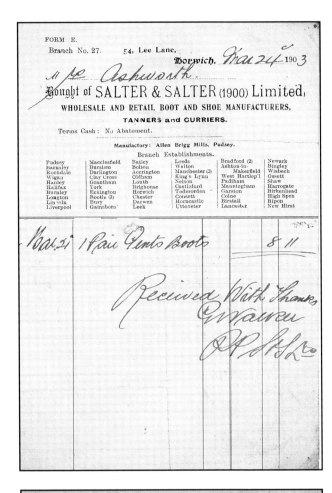

FORM E.
Branch No. 27.   54, Lee Lane,

Horwich. Mar 24 1903

Mr Ashworth.

Bought of **SALTER & SALTER** (1900) **Limited,**

WHOLESALE AND RETAIL BOOT AND SHOE MANUFACTURERS,

TANNERS and CURRIERS.

Terms Cash: No Abatement.

Manufactory: Allen Brigg Mills, Pudsey.

Branch Establishments.

Pudsey	Macclesfield	Batley	Leeds	Bradford (2)	Newark
Barnsley	Burslem	Bolton	Walton	Ashton-in-	Bingley
Rochdale	Darlington	Accrington	Manchester (3)	Makerfield	Wisbech
Wigan	Clay Cross	Oldham	King's Lynn	West Hartlep'l	Ossett
Hanley	Grantham	Louth	Nelson	Padiham	Shaw
Halifax	York	Brighouse	Castleford	Manningham	Harrogate
Burnley	Eckington	Horwich	Todmorden	Garston	Birkenhead
Longton	Bootle (2)	Chester	Consett	Colne	High Spen
Lincoln	Bury	Darwen	Horncastle	Birstall	Ripon
Liverpool	Gainsboro'	Leek	Uttoxeter	Lancaster	New Hirst

Mar 24 1 Pair Gents Boots   8 11

Received With Thanks,
G. Warner
p. Salter & Salter Ld

Mr. & Mrs. Peacock-Dyson who had a chemists' shop at 53 Lee Lane, Horwich. On the death of his wife, Mr. Peacock-Dyson paid for the erection of the lych-gate at Horwich Parish Church as a memorial to her.

Waddicor's cake shop, 33 Lee Lane, Horwich.

Mr. and Mrs. Waddicor, proprietors of the Lee Lane premises.

Houses numbered 54 to 60 Brownlow Road, Horwich, built by Mr. & Mrs. Waddicor.

Miss Bella Adamson's confectionery shop, 34 Winter Hey Lane, Horwich. 1925. Bella Adamson is standing to the left of the group.

Edward Brownlow & Sons, trade display stand at the Horwich Show, 1955.

E. Brownlow & Sons shop, 77 to 79 Lee Lane, Horwich. 1964.

Ferretti's ice-cream shop, Lee Lane, Horwich. 1965.

Riding's grocery store, Scholes Bank, Horwich. 1953.

Mrs. Riding with her son Peter, inside their shop on Scholes Bank, Horwich. Circa 1958.

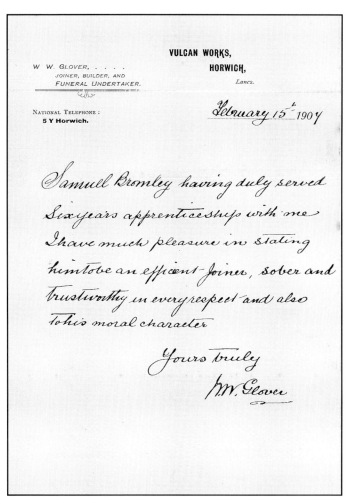

W. W. GLOVER, ...
JOINER, BUILDER, AND
FUNERAL UNDERTAKER.

VULCAN WORKS,
HORWICH,
Lancs.

NATIONAL TELEPHONE :
5 Y Horwich.

February 15ᵗ 1907

Samuel Bromley having duly served Six years apprenticeship with me I have much pleasure in stating him to be an efficient Joiner, sober and Trustworthy in every respect and also to his moral character

Yours truly

W. Glover

Reference supplied by W. W. Glover in respect of his apprentice, Samuel Bromley. 15th February 1907.

Mr. and Mrs. Sam Bromley who ran a joinery and undertaking business at 58 Brownlow Road, Horwich, photographed at their Silver Wedding in 1933.

145

Lee Lane, Horwich. Circa 1947. An extremely busy and interesting view of Lee Lane.

Ernest Hulme outside his Gents' Outfitters shop on Lee Lane, Horwich.

Horwich Utility Poultry shop, 110 Winter Hey Lane, Horwich. Circa 1960. Wilf Collins pictured inside his shop premises amongst the merchandise.

LIVESEY & SONS (HORWICH) LTD., FUNERAL DIRECTORS AND GARAGE PROPRIETORS, GORTON FOLD, HORWICH.

Gorton Fold Garage, Horwich. Circa 1930's. The building in the background top left is the Victoria Wesleyan Sunday School on Victoria Road.

Livesey's Wagonette. Circa 1920. Photograph taken outside Horwich Labour Club on Chorley New Road.

Livesey's Rolls Royce Hearse stands outside the Unitarian Chapel in Church Street, Horwich. Circa 1935.

Construction of Kwik Save Supermarket, Lee Lane, Horwich. 1964. The premises were built on the site of the old Prince's Theatre.

MOTOR VAN DELIVERIES DAILY.

H. GREGORY

NOTED FOR BEST IRISH BACON.

SMITH AND JONES

Lee Lane Post Office,

FOR

Irish Bacon and Ham—A.1.
Tinned Goods—Top Grade.

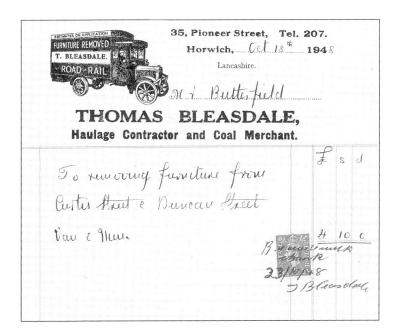

ESTIMATES ON APPLICATION
FURNITURE REMOVED
T. BLEASDALE.
ROAD · RAIL

35, Pioneer Street,   Tel. 207.
Horwich, *Oct 18ᵗʰ* 1948
Lancashire.

Mr. Butterfield

THOMAS BLEASDALE,

Haulage Contractor and Coal Merchant.

	£	s	d
To removing furniture from Curtis Street & Duncan Street Van & Men		4	10	0

LOCAL INNS AND BREWERS

Many of the licensed public houses in Horwich were supplied by local breweries, prominent amongst whom were John Sumner of Haigh and the Magee Marshall Brewery in Bolton. Horwich, in common with many northern industrial towns, was well served with licensed outlets. Several were built following the arrival of the locomotive works in the 1880's.

Sumner's off-licence, 45 Lee Lane, Horwich. Circia 1890.

William Barlow's Greenwood Inn, Chorley New Road, Horwich. Circa 1890.

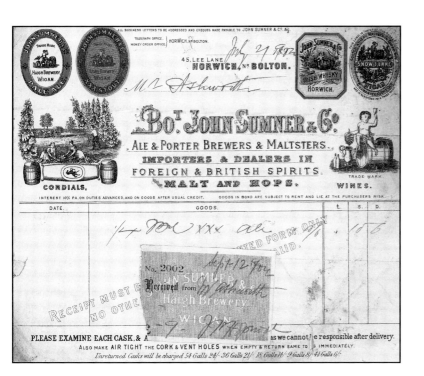

Invoice for ale bought from John Sumner & Co., 45 Lee Lane, Horwich. 1902.

Billiards game in progress at the Crown Inn, Horwich. Circa 1910.

Crown Inn, Horwich. Circa 1880.

Sawyer's Arms, Nelson Street, Horwich. Circa 1915.

Horwich Crown, Circa 1920. The Crown was a Magee Marshall's House, whilst the Queens Head Hotel was serviced by Nuttall's Brewery in Blackburn.

The Greenwood Hotel. Circa 1920. The Inn was re-built in the 1890's on a different site from its predecessor.
(see photo shown above.)

Rear of the Bee Hive Hotel, Horwich. Circa 1920.

The Squirrel Hotel on the Horwich / Anderton boundary. Burton Ales were the supplier of these premises. The hotel was demolished and re-built in the 1950's.

Scholes Bank Horwich. 1950. The property extream left is "Tottering Temple". The Squirrel Hotel is also visible on the left with the Water Board property on the right.

Coach trip from the Brown Cow in Church Street, Horwich. Circa 1950.

JOHN CRANKSHAW'S PIPEWORKS

John Crankshaw Co. Ltd., had extensive pipeworks situated at Old Lord's Height, Horwich, which were known locally as the 'Klondyke Pipeworks'. Clay and coal, which had been excavated from their local mines, was carried in tubs on a tramway to a 'tip shed' where it was stored in bunkers. The clay needed time to weather and when it was needed and ready for use it was loaded into buckets and carried by an overhead cableway to the pipeworks, where it was initially softened with water. The pipes which were manufactured were moulded by using steam presses and finally hardened in the kilns. At one time the pipes were glazed and made non-porous by using salt but this method created 'acid-rain' and was discontinued following numerous complaints. A method of slip-glazing was then introduced.

Production ceased at the works in the early 1980's and the whole complex, including the kilns, was eventually demolished. In August 1980, whilst the pipeworks were under demolition, Paul Barry Mason took a series of photographs at the site and the results, some of which are included below, show what a large industrial concern the works represented and provide an interesting record of Horwich's industrial past.

The office accommodation is on the extreme left of this photograph, the kilns are in the centre and the buildings on the right comprise the mill house, pipe presses and drying bays, the canteen and the blacksmiths' shop.

On the reverse of this photograph is written, 'Gladys - Klondyke'. It shows Gladys Calvert (nee Leech) holding her pet dog with John Crankshaw's works in the background. Circa 1950.

View of the kilns in front of the drying shed. The steel ducting carried heat to the drying shed thus removing the need for the old Lancashire Boilers.

The entrance to the kiln is visible and this would be sealed when the kilns were fired.

Close-up view of Kiln No. 7.

The tramway from the mine to the works once ran along the back of the kilns where what appears to be a footway, can be seen.

In the centre of the photograph can be seen the top of one of the old pipe presses.

John Garrity, who worked at the pipeworks, recognised the large bow-saw in this bay of the drying shed as the one he used during his employ. The plastic sheeting on the floor was used to cover pipe bends to prevent their drying out too quickly and cracking.

This shows the remains of one of the upstairs drying bays at the works.

The building on the left of this photograph was used to service / repair vehicles belonging to the company.

Two general views showing the structure and the arrangement of the kilns.

ASSOCIATED CLAY INDUSTRIES, LIMITED.

PRODUCTION BONUS SCHEME.

(1) Subject to conditions outlined below Production Bonus is payable in respect to all hours worked at normal day-work rates. No bonus is payable in respect of overtime or other hours involving rates above normal or in respect of piece-work operations.

(2) Any employee losing time which involves the deduction of more than four "quarters" or a total of more than one hour in any pay week forfeits bonus for that week.

(3) Bonus forfeited is "pooled" and distributed by increasing proportionately the bonus rate payable to those qualifying.

(4) Bonus is based on total output ex kiln less all breakages and scrap during the pay week and on the total Paid Man Hours for that week.

(5) Total weight ex kiln is recorded first in Nominal Tons based on A.C.I. Standard Weight List.

(6) Since Nominal Tons vary considerably in value according to the proportion of Fittings etc., it is necessary to eliminate this by converting Nominal Tons to Unit Tons as follows:

    1 Nominal Ton of Best Pipes   = 1.0 Unit Ton.
    1   "   " of Seconds Pipes   = 0.8   "   "
    1   "   " of Best Fittings(Moulded)= 3.0   "   "
    1   "   " of Secs   "   "   = 2.4   "   "

(7) Actual Man Hours worked are converted to Paid Man Hours by adding extra hours paid as overtime.

(8) The number of Paid Man Hours per ton for a particular pay week is found by dividing the total number of Paid Man Hours by the nett output for that week in Unit Tons.

(9) Each Week, basic figures calculated as above are given in respect of

        (a) Total nett production for that week in Unit Tons
        (b) Total number of Paid Man Hours.
        (c) Number of Paid Man Hours per Unit Ton.

(10) To determine Bonus payable, note on the graph the point at which the horizontal line indicating the number of Paid Man Hours per Unit Ton crosses the diagonal showing the Weekly Production in Unit Tons. The vertical line nearest this point then gives the Bonus payable to within one tenth of one penny per hour.

(11) The Company reserves the right to modify or withdraw this Bonus Scheme on giving four weeks notice accordingly.

12th February, 1948.

Manager.
ASSOCIATED CLAY INDUSTRIES Ltd
CRANKSHAW WORKS.

Details of the production bonus scheme operative at the works.

MONTCLIFFE MINE

John Garrity, a Horwich man, worked in Montcliffe Colliery which was known locally as the Pottery Coalpit. It was one of the last few privately owned mines to be operated in the Bolton area. John recorded his experiences in two interesting booklets from which, with his permission, the following information has been obtained.

Montcliffe Colliery had two shafts with winding gear, No. 1 shaft - sunk in 1820 to a depth of 400 yards, and No. 2 shaft - sunk in 1860 to a depth of 365 yards. When the second shaft was sunk, No. 1 Shaft ceased to be used other than for ventilation to the workings and as a means of escape in emergency.

From 1864 until 1882 the mine was not worked but Herbert Mason eventually re-opened the workings. Initially, clay was used from the 'Marjery' seam to make bricks, which were of poor quality and did not sell well. A quantity did however sell at 54/- per 1000, which were used to construct Horwich Police Station in 1886 / 87.

An extremely dry spell during 1887 led to a critical water shortage and the Horwich Local Board was forced to consider options to resolve the situation. Blackrod Reservoir was the main source of supply and Horwich obtained a 50,000 gallon daily supply for which Blackrod Local Board was paid sixpence per 1000 gallons.

Montcliffe Mine, in common with most other underground operations, had a problem with water in the workings. No. 1 Shaft, it will be remembered, was sunk in 1820 to a depth of 400 yards and it was the water accumulation in some of the abandoned workings at a depth of 490 ft which eventually provided a solution. Following exhaustive testing, the water from the mine workings was adjudged to be of excellent quality, principally due to the natural filtration achieved by travelling through thick beds of sandstone. It was possible, at very little expense, to obtain a daily supply of up to 358,000 gallons at a cost of three pence halfpenny per 1,000 gallons; even cheaper than that supplied by Blackrod. In the event, the proposed scheme was adopted by Horwich Local Board. An underground reservoir held about 30,000 gallons of water which was connected to the town's supply system.

The construction of Horwich Locomotive Works from 1886 meant a sharp rise in the population of Horwich and the extra demands for water meant that the new supply was destined to remain.

While the water supply scheme was in operation No. 2 Shaft at Montcliffe Mine was sunk to an even greater depth to access the lower coal / clay seams. No. 1 Shaft then reverted to being used for ventilation and escape. Tubs of coal and clay mined were wound up the No. 2 shaft, weighed, and then lowered along a tramway to be unloaded into bunkers near the No. 1 Shaft. Steam engines constantly operated to provide the motive power at the mine and, in addition, cottages at White Gate were heated on the tenants paying a few pennies per week for the supply of steam from the mine engines.

During the 1950's Montcliffe Colliery employed some 26 men. This number was made up by the manager, a surface banksman, winder, fireman, two surface tippers, a pit bottom onsetter, and nineteen colliers and drawers. The working seam was five to six feet high. The face roughly consisted of a bottom seam of coal 9" to 18", a seam of fire clay about 18", a band of dirt varying in thickness with a further 12" seam of coal on top.

Wages for underground workers were £6.50p per day with the opportunity to raise it to £10 per day by increasing the output. Mining was ever a dangerous occupation and conditions at Montcliffe Mine were little different than in the Nationalised industry except that expediency to make profit sometimes resulted in safety procedures and operating instructions being ignored.

No. 1 Shaft had a wooden headstock which was declared unsafe by H.M. Inspector of Mines during the early 1960s. Instead of sinking a new shaft a drift tunnel was constructed to the surface with a 1 in 3 gradient, which was the cheaper option.

WILDERSMOOR DRIFT MINE

Coal and clay was extracted from the Wildersmoor Drift Mine by the 'pillar and stall' method. Basically, sections of the coal seam were left unworked to act as roof supports. The coal and clay extracted was placed into tubs and wheeled along rails to be emptied outside the mine. An empty tub was then returned to the face-worker. There were two sections to the Wildersmoor Drift Mine known respectively as the 'Little Mine' and the 'Big Mine'. The former ran underneath the 'Sportsman's Cottage' and came to the surface near the Rivington boundary. The latter junctioned from the 'Little Mine' and employed up to eleven men and boys. A system of piece-work was in operation (2/6d per tub). Entry could be obtained to the Big Mine from Wildersmoor. Shot-firing with gelignite dislodged the coal and clay and it was necessary to use bars and pit-props to secure the roof every three feet, which practice was known as 'timbering' in addition to the pillar and stall procedure.

The mine was in operation until 1961.

Wildersmoor Drift Mine tramway. 1995.

Entrance to Wildersmoor Drift Mine.
(Photo courtesy of John Garrity.)

The spoil heap and powder magazine for the mine are visible centre. 1995.

From left to right - Beris Foy, John Lewis and John Garrity near to the air shafts on Wildersmoor. 1960.

Amongst the miners are - P. Moss, R. Adamson, B. Armstrong and Mr. Jackson.
(Photo courtesy of John Garrity.)

Middle-wheel and smithy, Wildersmoor Colliery, Horwich. Circa 1960.
(Photo courtesy of John Garrity.)

Pictured in the Big Mine at Wildersmoor Colliery are front (left to right) Roy Adamson (Deputy) and Neil Broadbent. Rear (left to right) Ted Stuchbury, Bill Adamson, Harold Bullough and Walter Phillips.

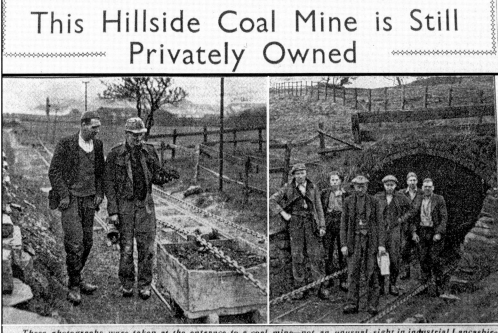

This Hillside Coal Mine is Still Privately Owned

These photographs were taken at the entrance to a coal mine—not an unusual sight in industrial Lancashire—but this is a mine with a difference, for it is one of the few privately-owned coal producers in the country, and certainly the only one in this district. Wildersmoor Mine, just a hole in the bleak hillside below Rivington Pike to local people, is almost a coal mine by accident. Owned by the Associated Clay Industries, Ltd., its chief function is the mining of first-quality fireclay, with an average yield of 300 tons weekly, but it also produces about 50 tons of good quality coal, each week, and is licensed by the National Coal Board. There are two seams, with 50 miners employed, and the workings extend approximately one mile and run alongside Scotchman's Stump. The mine is of considerable age, but was first worked extensively upon the appointment of the present manager, Mr. R. Adamson, in 1915.

The men shown in the newspaper article - first picture on left - Jim Stuchbury and Mo. Heyes. Group in right hand picture (left to right) Ted Stuchbury, Jack Armstrong, Jack Rawlinson, Tommy Ingram, Bob Fitton and Harold Bullough.

QUARRIES

Lying on a spur of the Pennine Chain the underlying rock of the Horwich District has proved a valuable source of material for both building and road making. Several disused quarries appear on the old maps including the Ridgeway Delf, Tup Row Quarry and Pilkington Quarry. In the Directory of Quarries, Clayworks & Sand & Gravel Pits, Etc., 1943 - 44 edition; Jas. Nuttall & Son (Horwich) Ltd., appear as the owners of what is presently known as Montcliffe Quarry. Stone is extracted by means of explosives and siren warning is given when blasting is about to start. The quarrying of rock is a skilled and labour intensive operation and it is pleasing to be afforded the opportunity to include photographs of the industry many of which belong personally to Eric Stuchbury of Tomlinson Street, Horwich.

This advertising blotter issued by Thomas Finch & Sons, Pilkington Quarry, Horwich, indicates that stone from the quarry was used in the construction of Bolton Town Hall during 1888.

QUARRY WORKING IN THE LATE 1950'S and EARLY 1960'S

A Weatherill loading shovel, loading waste sand into a wagon. On the left is the conveyor belt, taking stone from the main crusher to the secondary crusher.

164

Neil Weaver driving a Weatherill loader. The building on the left is the main crusher house. On the right is a conveyor going to 'Middle Bunkers' and 'Top Bunkers'.

Excavator loading stone from the main face of the quarry onto a 'Leyland Comet' Wagon.

Eric Stuchbury driving a 'Foden' wagon after tipping stone into the main crusher.

This photograph shows the main face in the quarry. On the top is a Ruston Bucyrus 24RB Excavator. Below can be seen a Ruston Bucyrus 22RB Excavator and a Weatherill loader.

John Stuchbury and Quarry Wagon.

A Ruston Bucyrus 19RB Excavator at Montcliffe Stone Quarry.

Jim Stuchbury with a 'Leyland' Quarry wagon.

A Ruston Bucyrus 22RB mechanical shovel loading stone into a dump truck to be transported to the main crusher.

Montcliffe Quarry employees 1958 / 59. Back Row (left to right) Bernard Fairclough, Bill Fairbanks, Jack Grimes, Jimmy Drakely, Neil Weaver and Jim Stuchbury. Front Row (left to right) Sam Pilkington, Ken Whittaker, Harry Fletcher.

Montcliffe Quarry. Circa 1990. The main drill and compressor are visible to the left and are in the process of drilling holes for the explosives prior to blasting. The usual time for detonation of the charges was 12 noon prior to which a siren was sounded as a safety warning.

Montcliffe Quarry. Circa 1990. The main crusher house and the conveyor belt system can be seen to the right, while the crane jib on the left belonged to a drop-ball excavator used for reducing boulders which were too large for the crusher.

BOY SCOUTS AND GIRL GUIDES

The Boy Scouts movement was founded in 1908 by Lord Baden-Powell and the Girl Guides came into existence in 1910. They have since become world wide movements and Horwich has played an active part in promoting the aims of the two organisations.

Horwich Scouts. Circa 1910.

2nd Horwich Girl Guide Company. 1920.

I have had the pleasure of examining two log books relating to Horwich and District Boy Scouts Local Association meetings, from their inauguration on the 29th June 1910 to the 29th June 1931; along with the 4th Horwich Scout troop log book from its registration on the 15th December 1915 until the 15th June 1930. The two books make fascinating reading and extracts are included below. There are also two trophies in existence which were presented in relation to scouting activities.

The Coleman Challenge Shield. At a meeting held on the 30th September 1912, in the Scouts' Clubroom at Horwich, Miss Coleman, daughter of the late Reverend G.W. Coleman, offered a challenge shield to be competed for by scouts of the district troops. The disciplines involved in the competition were Ambulance, Path-Finding, Signalling and Cookery. Two winners are recorded on the shield, the 1st Horwich in 1914-1915 and the 4th Horwich during the 1918-1919 competition.

The Slingsby Memorial Football Cup. This trophy was competed for annually by local scouts.
It is inscribed as follows:
Presented to the
HORWICH BOY SCOUTS ASSOCIATION by
Scoutmaster Harold W. Jackson,
IN AFFECTIONATE MEMORY
OF COMMISSIONER ANTHONY SLINGSBY
AND OUR LOCAL SCOUTS KILLED IN ACTION
IN THE GREAT WAR.
1915
Scoutmasters H. TATLOW. N. BIRCHALL
1916
Patrol Leader G. DEWHURST
Scout " H.L. JACKSON.
1917
Patrol Leader A. Powell
Scout " P. HOLDEN.

On the plinth is engraved:
THE
SLINGSBY MEMORIAL
FOOTBALL CUP

In the Secretary's Annual Report of the Horwich and District Boy Scouts Local Association, compiled by their Hon Secretary, Miss M. Coleman, is the following paragraph:- "Immediately on the declaration of war, our Scouts were mobilised as far as private circumstances permitted, and their services offered to the Chief Constable of Lancashire, the Horwich and Blackrod Urban District Councils, and the local Ambulance authorities, with the result that Scouts were employed to guard the Horwich Waterworks and gathering grounds until the appointment of suitable watchmen for the purpose, while others were able to make themselves useful to the different regiments of Territorials, who encamped for a short time in Lever Park during the process of mobilisation.

Coleman Shield Competition, winning team 1918 - 1919. The winning team comprised, Senior Patrol Leader A.W. Sleigh, Senior Scout F. Offord, Patrol Leader H. Foster, Patrol Leader J. Wolfe and Patrol Leader E. Hawksworth (reserve). Miss Rigby of Preston, who appears in the photograph, also presented gold centre medals to the members of the successful team.

Among the log books for Horwich Scouts was this interesting photograph of a uniformed scout. The background to the picture has not been identified but is thought to be local.

A Scout Rally was held on the Horwich R.M.I. Recreation Ground on the 9th September 1916 during which the photographs shown below were taken.

Scout Rally, September 9th 1916 at Horwich R.M.I Recreation Ground.

AT THE GOING DOWN OF THE SUN

Involvement in two World Wars was often brought home to the local populace most vividly when reports were received from the various theatres of conflict of the death or serious injury of relatives and friends. Many of the obituary notices relating to the First World War, 1914 to 1918, are particularly poignant in that they highlight the youth of the fatal casualties and leave the unanswered question of why a particular father or son had to perish. It is the general rule of life that in peacetime sons bury their fathers but in wartime the situation is often that fathers bury their sons. Many young Horwich men made the supreme sacrifice.

Horwich has thus been burdened with its share of sacrifice for the common good of mankind and it is incumbent upon us to ensure that we remember those who fell in battle fighting the 'good' fight. The town has several sites for remembrance including the main cenotaph at the junction of Scholes Bank and Lever Park Avenue; and the memorial to those employees at Horwich Locomotive Works who perished during the two world wars. In addition, many of the schools and churches erected their own memorials and one is also maintained in the Public Hall on Lee Lane.

The following series of illustrations is intended to present a cameo of how directly these and other conflicts have affected the people of the district.

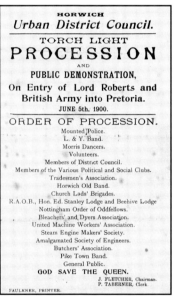

First World War soldiers outside Horwich Drill Hall, Longworth Road, Horwich.
Circa 1916.

Sapper Edward Leech, Signal Section Royal Engineers, 60th Infantry Brigade, photographed with his father John Thomas Leech. Photo by Ralph Close of Horwich.

Sapper Leech's brother, Thomas Edward Leech of the 4th Battalion Loyal North Lancashire Regiment was killed in action at the Battle of Festubert on the 15th June 1915.

John Thomas Leech with his dog Toby outside his home in Leicester Avenue, Horwich. Circa 1910.

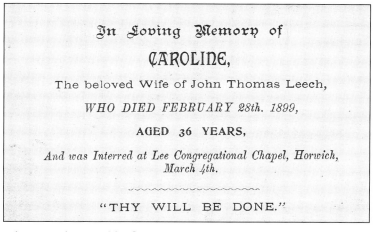

In memoriam card for Sapper Leech's mother Caroline who died in 1899 aged 36 years.

CERTIFIED COPY of an ENTRY of BIRTH.

Superintendent Registrar's District of _Bolton_

Registrar's Sub-District of _Horwich_ in the Count _y_ of _Lancaster_

No.	When and where Born.	Name (if any).	Sex.	Name and Surname of Father.	Name and Maiden Surname of Mother.	Rank or Profession of Father.	Signature, Description, and Residence of Informant.	When Registered.	Signature of Registrar.	Baptismal Name, if added after Registration of Birth.
385	Twenty fourth June 1890 25 Dickenson Street East Horwich U.S.d	Edward	Boy	John Thomas Leech	Caroline Leech formerly Attwood	Steam Engine Fitter (Journeyman)	Caroline Leech Mother 25 Dickenson Street East Horwich	Fourteenth August 1890	Ralph Bates Registrar	

I hereby certify that the above is a true Copy of an Entry of Birth in a Register Book in my custody.

Witness my hand this _6_ day of _November_ 19_03_

[signature]

Superintendent Registrar.
25, Mawdsley Street, Bolton.

[NOTE.—The word "Superintendent" to be prefixed to "Registrar" when the Certificate is given by the Superintendent Registrar.]

270ce)

Copy of Birth Certificate and Labour Certificate for Edward LEECH-

---

FOR CHILDREN BETWEEN THIRTEEN AND FOURTEEN YEARS OF AGE ONLY.

BOARD OF EDUCATION.
Form 146 (a).

SCHEDULE III.

School District of _HORWICH._

LABOUR CERTIFICATE, No. 1.

AGE AND EMPLOYMENT.

I certify that _Edward Leach_ residing at _14 Emmett St_ Horwich, was, on the _16th_ day of _June_ 19_03_, not less than **twelve** years of age, having been born on the _3rd_ day of _June_ 18_90_ as appears by the Registrar's Certificate [or the Statutory Declaration] now produced to me, (¹) and has been shown to the satisfaction of the local authority for this district to be beneficially employed.

(Signed) _G S Ainsworth_

(¹) Clerk to the (¹) SCHOOL ATTENDANCE OFFICER.

for the above district.

(¹) Strike out what follows if the child is qualified for full time employment.

(¹) or other officer.
(²) School Board or School Attendance Committee.

W. B. & L. (135cs)—2196s—20000-5-1900

PROFICIENCY.

SCHEDULE VI.

Education Department
Form No. 144 (c).

Certificate of School Attendance for the purpose of employment under Section 5, Elementary Education Act, 1876.

[School]

I hereby certify that the following particulars in respect to the Attendances made by the Child named below, at this School, after attaining the age of 5 years, are correctly taken from the Registers of the School.

Name in full, and Residence of Child	Number of Attendances made within the 12 months ending the 31st December
Edward Leach, 14 Emmett St, Horwich.	1897. 408 1898. 399 1899. 417 1900. 404 1901. 406

Signed this _20 JUN 1902_ day of

Chas H Field

Principal Teacher of the above-named School.

* Enter name in full, and state whether a Public Elementary, or Certified Efficient School.

Printed for H.M. Stationery Office by W. P. Griffith, Ltd., 34, Bloomfield, E.C.

Horwich Company of the Loyal North Lancs Regiment.

KILLED.

Sgt. G. F. KIRKMAN.   Sgt. JOHN BIBBY.

Sergt. Geo. F. KIRKMAN, King's Liverpool Regiment, eldest son of Mr. Reuben Kirkman, 33, Lever Edge-lane, Great Lever, died in Neath Military Hospital on Monday from influenza. He had seen three years' service, being wounded on the Somme 18 months ago, and after recovering became Sergeant-in-Charge of Port Talbot Prisoners of War Camp. He was a member of the Great Lever Golf Club, and his name is on the Rolls of Honour at the Central Higher Grade School and Bolton Conservative Club. He will be interred at Heaton Cemetery to-day.

Sergt. JOHN BIBBY (23), Lancashire Fusiliers, a former employee of the Star Bleaching Co., Horwich, died of wounds on November 9th, 1918. He enlisted soon after the outbreak of war in September, 1914. His

Pte. S. H. THORPE.   Pte. J. FLAHERTY.

Pte. SAMUEL HERBERT THORPE, of the 3rd King's Liverpool Regiment, was interred in the Horwich Parish Churchyard on Nov. 14th, death having been caused by pneumonia following on influenza. Private Thorpe formerly resided with his parents at 4, Latham-row, Horwich, and joined the Army in September, 1914, when he was employed as a boot and shoe maker at Southport. Aged 24, he was a member of the Chapel-in-the-Fields congregation. His name appears on the Roll of Honour at the Old Boys' School, Horwich, where deceased was educated.

Pte. JACK FLAHERTY (20), L.N.L. Regiment, whose parents live at 373, Lever-st., was killed on October 1st. He first went to France 17 months ago. Prior to enlisting he was a minder employed by Messrs. Crosses and Winkworth, Ltd., and his name is on the Roll of Honour at St. Mark's Church.

Reports of local men killed in action or receiving military honours regularly appeared in the newspapers throughout the 1914 / 1918 War. The entries shown appeared in the Bolton Journal and Guardian on Friday, November 29th 1918.

James Hampson and his wife at their wedding. He was employed as a chargehand pattern maker at Horwich Locomotive Works and is referred to on the Roll of Honour for Horwich Old Boys' School.

Ted and Lily Leech's wedding at St. Catherine's Church, Horwich. 1919.

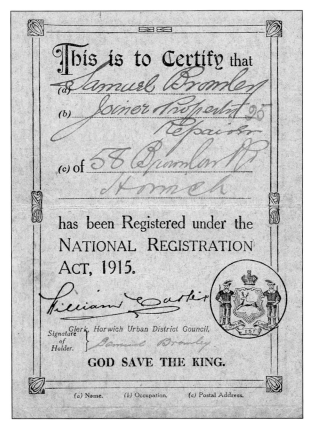

National Registration Card for Samuel Bromley, 58 Brownlow Road, Horwich.

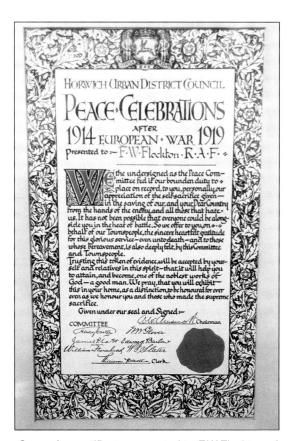

Copy of a certificate presented to F.W.Flockton of the Royal Air Force by the Peace Committee of Horwich Urban District Council as a token of the town's esteem for his war services.

*Makinson's munition workers, 1914 - 1918 World War.
The premises pictured were situated in Winter Hey Lane.*

*Horwich Branch of the Discharged Soldiers and Sailors Committee. 1922.
This group were instrumental in the formation of Horwich British Legion.*

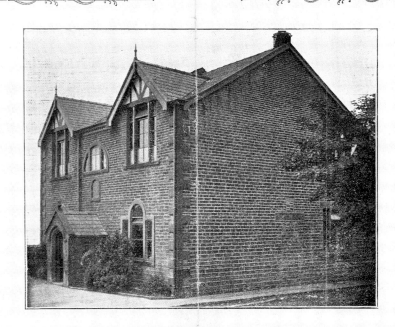

THE GREAT WAR.

Roll of Honour. Horwich Old Boys' School.

September, 1915.

Dear Boys,

It is very gratifying that so many of my former pupils have responded to call of King and Country. "The Boys" of the Old School will I am sure do their duty, and they have the prayers of the present teachers and scholars that they may do "well" and return happily.

This Roll may not be complete, but any error or omission you may point out will be corrected in a future list. It is proposed to put up an illuminated framed copy in the school.

I should be pleased to receive your photo to add to the Roll.

Yours faithfully,

T. H. H. BUCKLEY.

H. FLETCHER, PRINTER, HORWICH.

. ROLL OF HONOUR. .

	Ashcroft, John	...3rd E. L. R. F. A...	...Saddler, 1304.
	Archer, Frank	...170th R. F. A.	...Driver, 17679.
	Abbott, Richard	... "	...Private.
Discharged	Abbott, William	...County Pals Art.	...Private, 10548.
	Alderman, Walter	...8th L. N. L.	...Private, 19658.
	Abbott, Stanley	...R. G. A.	...Gunner, 55775.
	Adamson, Tom	...A. S. C. Motor Tran.	Private, 104001.
	Abbott, John	...H.M.S. Argyle	...
Discharged	Barlow, Timothy	...4th L. N. L.	...Drummer, 2410.
	Belfield, William	...9th Batt. K.O.R.L.	...Private, 14212.
	Belfield, James A.	...1/4 L. N. L. (Sig.)	...Lance Corp.264.
	Brownlow, Joseph	...149th R. F. A.	...Driver, 16511.
	Bromilow, Wilfred	...170th R. F. A.	...Private, 17680.
	Butler, George	...3rd E. L.	...Private, 16696.
	Bishop, William B.	...Kent Batt.	...Private, 2649.
	Boardman, Stanley	...3/2th E. L. F. A.	...Private, 684.
Killed	Birchall, Theodore	...H.M.S. Warrior	...Stoker.
	Butterworth, John	...1/5th L. N. L.	...Private, 2505.
	Butterworth Fredk.	...10th Kings Liverpool	Private, 4343.
		(Scottish)	
	Butterworth, William	do.	...Private, 5094.
	Briggs, Harold	...5th L. N. L.	...Private, 2685.
	Beddows, John	...1/1 W. L. D. (R.E.)	...Signaller, 6974.
	Bromilow, Peers	...170th R. F. A.	...Driver, 17678.
KILLED	Bromilow, Daniel	...3rd King's Own R. L.	Private, 18644.
	Cooper, Fred	...5th L. N. L.	...Private, 2336.
	Cooper, Herbert A.	...11th L. N. L.	...Sergeant, 17236.
	Clare, Leonard	...67th Field Co. R. E.	...Sapper, 45766.
	Colvin, James	...4th L. N. L.	...Private, 2400.
	Calderbank, Harry	... "	...Private, 1645.
	Calderbank, John B.	R. E.	...Sapper, 9139.
	Cotton, Stanley	20th Royal Fus.	Private, 6616.
WOUNDED	Clayton, Stanley	...4th L. N. L.	...Sergeant, 1284.
	Chipchase, Jesse	...3rd E. L. R. F. A.	...Gunner, 921.
	Caldwell, Mitchell	...3rd L. N. L.	...Sergeant.
	Danks, William	...H.M.S. Hodder,Tran.	Engineer.
	Dent, Adam	...21st Canadians	...Private, 629.
	Dutton, Sidney	...2/6 Manchesters	...Private, 2947.
	Davies, Albert	...3rd Devons	...Private, 16157.
	Davies, Evan	...171st R. F. A.	...Driver, 17831.
	Dale, George	...8th L. N. L.	...Private, 1627.
	Davies, Ernest	...Royal Naval Res.	...
	Davenport, George	...R. A. M. C.	...Private, 54632.
	Davenport, Richard	...R. E.	...Lnce Cor.51670.
	Davenport, Tom	...L. N. L.	...Private, 17498.
	Ellison, Thomas	...4th L. N. L.	...Private, 1638.
	France, Herbert	...20th R. F. A.	...Private, 55722.
	Ferrier, Harold	...A. S. C.	...Corp. (L.H.), 035908.
	Gill, John	...3rd L. N. L.	...Private, 19371.
	Gill, Thomas	...10th L. N. L.	...Private, 15455.
	Gill, Stanley	...South Wales Bord.	...Private, 24671.
	Gorman, Joseph	...R. Anglesea R. E.	...Sapper, 7620.
	Gerrard, Tom	...11th Aus. Exp. F.	...Private, 276.
	Gill, Paul	...10th L. N. L.	...Private.
	Haslam, George	...R. A. R. E.	...Private, 7561.
	Hunt, Tom	...A.S.C. Motor Trans.	...Corporal, 1826.
	Hopwood, Henry	...Royal Engineers	...Sapper, 7629.
KILLED June 27-1916.	Hodgkinson, James	...10th L. N. L.	...Corporal,14717.
	Hampson, James	...4th L. N. L.	...Sergeant, 886.
	Hill, John	...5th L. N. L.	...Private, 4562.
KILLED	Haslam, Frank	...1st Batt. Scots Grds.	...Private, 9528.
	Hawkesworth, Geo.	1/4th L. N. L.	...Private, 1618.
KILLED	Hornby, Henry	...8th L. N. L.	...Scout, 16294.
Died of wounds.	Hart, Fred	...10th L. N. L.	...Private, 14720.
	Ironfield, Albert	..R. E.	...Sapper, 7631.

Jones, Richard E.	...15th S.B.Welsh Reg.	...Private, 20697.	
Jolly, Horace	...R. F. A.	...Driver, 24453.	
Jolly, Frank	...8th L. N. L.	...Signaller, 14410.	
Jolly, Fred	...8th L. N. L.	...Private, 14406.	
Jones, Ernest	...61st Batt. R. F. A.	...Gunner, 73836.	
Jackson, William	...1/4th L. N. L.	...Private, 277.	
Kirkman, Harry	...10th L. N. L.	...Private, 14409.	
Kirkman, Fred	...R. F. A.	...Driver, 1904.	
Longworth, Arthur	...10th L. N. L.	...Private, 14719.	*WOUNDED*
Longworth, Albert E.	17th S. B. L. (King's Own)	...Lnce Cor, 15272.	*wounded*
Lowe, James	...K. R. R.	...Private, 8599.	
Lacey, Thomas	...4/5 L. N. L.	...Private, 5358.	
Landless, James	...7th Manc. Reg.	...Private, 20937.	
Makinson, James B.	...3rd L. N. L.	...Private, 19790.	
Marsden, Thomas	...15th Can. Highlndrs.	Private, 77731.	
McGregor, Thomas	...L. N. L.	...Private, 15325.	
Mather, John	...13th L. F.	...Private, 13598.	
McManus, Thomas	...W. L. Cyclists Div.	... 257.	
Plant, Arthur	...Lanc. Fusiliers	...Private, 6650.	
Pendlebury, Thos. H.	L. N. L.	...Signaller, 14718.	
Partington, Herbert	...10th L. N. L.	...Private, 14408.	
Palmer, Harry	...4th L. N. L.	...Private, 1644.	
Pollitt, Fred	...3rd K. O. R. L.	...Private, 18404.	
Ryder, Thomas	...10th L. N. L.	...Private, 14407.	*Killed*
Ryder, Charles	...169th R. F. A.	...Private, 17220.	
Rangeley, Frank	...8th L. N. L.	...Private, 19657.	
Rutherford, Harry	...2/10th L. N. L.	...Private, 1402.	
Shorrocks, Thomas	...20th Royal Fus.	...Private, 7062.	
Smith, William	...9th K. O. R. Lanc.	...Private, 14226.	
Smith, Harry	...9th K. O. R. Lanc.	...Private, 14225.	
Shawcross, Charles	...7th Canadians	...	
Stones, Robert	...1/4th L. N. L.	...Lance Cor. 1643.	*KILLED*
Stones, Philip	...2/3rd E. L. R. F. A.	...Gunner, 1776.	*Wounded*
Sutton, Joseph	...1st Gordon High.	...Private, 10232.	
Simm, William	...Lanc. Fusiliers	...Private, 7459.	
Sefton, John	...8th L. N. L.	...Private, 14716.	*KILLED*
Seddon, Edward	...R. A. M. C.	...Private, 58782.	
Taylor, Arnold	...R. A. M. C.	...Private, 54599.	
Taylor, Frank	...County Pals R. E.	...Private, 81822.	
Tetlow, Z. Stanley	...M. T. A. S. C.	...Private, 119683.	
Thorpe, Herbert	...12th King's L. R.	...Private, 18795.	
Tomkinson, Frank	...12th Lanc. Fusiliers	Drummer, 6627.	
Tomkinson, Cornelius	R. G. A.	...Private, 55912.	
Tetlow, Harold	...A.S.C. Mec. Trans.	...Private, 1262.	
Thomas, Horace	...2nd Lanc. Fusiliers	...Private, 3106.	
Walsh, Christopher	...10th L. N. L.	...Private, 14366.	
Walsh, Joseph	...3rd Batt. L. N. L.	...Private, 19313.	
Walsh, Albert	...5th L. N. L.	...Private, 4352.	
Wilde, Edgar	...R. G. A.	...	
Williams, Frank	...L. N. L.	...Private, 14376.	
Williams, Harry	...10th L. N. L.	...Private, 14363.	
Williams, Harry	...165th Batt. R.F.A.	...Private, 10628.	
Walsh, Fred	...Royal Flying Corps	Private, 6248.	
Wood, William	...	...	
Walkden, Fred	...R. E.	...Signaller, 50158.	
Whittaker, Ernest	...15th A. S. C.	...Private, 2511.	
Yardley, Percy	...3rd E. L. R. F. A.	...Private, 1905.	*DISCHARGED*

SICK BERTH RESERVE, R. N.

Farnworth, Walter	...	...rd Master.	
Ferrier, Charles E.	...	...vate.	
Ellison, Joseph	...	...rivate.	

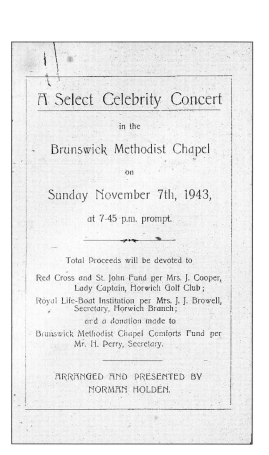

A Select Celebrity Concert

in the

Brunswick Methodist Chapel

on

Sunday November 7th, 1943,

at 7-45 p.m. prompt.

Total Proceeds will be devoted to

Red Cross and St. John Fund per Mrs. J. Cooper, Lady Captain, Horwich Golf Club;

Royal Life-Boat Institution per Mrs. J. J. Browell, Secretary, Horwich Branch;

and a donation made to Brunswick Methodist Chapel Comforts Fund per Mr. H. Perry, Secretary.

ARRANGED AND PRESENTED BY
NORMAN HOLDEN.

PROGRAMME.

1. Irene Goodram and her Accordion
   (a) In a Monastery Garden ... Albert W. Ketelbey.
   (b) The Lost Chord ... ... A. Sullivan.

2. Horwich Senior Girls' School Choir
   by kind permission of Miss D. H. Green, B.A.
   Conductor ... Miss M. Calderwood.
   Accompanist ... Madam Harrison.
   (a) Song of the Waters   part   Rathbone
   (b) Let the Bright Seraphim   unison   Handel
   (c) The Galway Piper   three part   Irish Air arranged by Percy Fletcher
   (d) Comfort Ye, My People   Recitative
   (e) O Thou that tellest good   three part   From Handel's tidings   " Messiah."

3. Jimmy Beatty and His Violin
   Accompanist—Mrs. J. Bain, A.L.C.M.
   (a) Romantic Piece   Dvorak
   (b) Praeludium and Allegro   G. Pugnai - Kreisler

4. Victor Hardman, Cpl. R.A.F.
   Impressions of leading personalities including Winston Churchill, F. D. Roosevelt, the late John Hilton.
   Prior to "Ack-Ack, Beer-Beer," Monday, Nov. 8th, 1943.

5. Rita and Sheila Hazlehurst
   Piano and Cornet Selections.
   (a) The Rose of Tralee.
   (b) Son of My Soul.

6. PERCY MANCHESTER
   Star of over 400 Broadcasts
   Radio Maestro of Song, singing the Songs you love.
   At the piano LOUISE.

7. Keith Bond   Pianoforte Solo
   (a) Selections from "French Suites"   Bach
   (b) The Towing Path   John Ireland
   (c)—Andante (Sonata No. 10)   Beethoven

8. Sallie Markland   Soprano
   (a) Lo! Here the Gentle Lark   Sir Henry Bishop
   (b) I Hear You Calling Me   Charles Marshall
   (c) Sing, Joyous Bird   Montague F. Phillips
   Accompanist—Helen Hindley Smith.

9. Norman Wright   'Cello Solos
   (a) Danse Orientale   Squire
   (b) Le Cygne (The Swan)   Saint-Saëns
   (c) Chanson Villageoise   Popper
   Accompanist—Ethel Greenhalgh, L.T.C.M.

10. TURNER LAYTON at the Piano
    RADIO and Stage STAR.

Stage Manager ... Sydney Hanson.

APPRECIATION.

To all who have assisted me in the organising of the Concert, especially the Artists who have given their services entirely free, W. Haydock, A. E. Perry, H. & J. Kenyon, F. Abbott, F. Roberts, J. Marsden, G. Wilford, Trustees of Brunswick Methodist Chapel and all who have assisted in any way to making this effort a great success.

Yours truly,
NORMAN HOLDEN.

Sisters Lily (left) and Ethel Leech of Horwich, in uniform during the 1940's.

Bomb damage in Lever Park Avenue, Horwich, during the 1939 -1945 World War.

War memorial outside the old Horwich Locomotive Works. 1990.

Horwich's Garden of Remembrance situated at the junction of Scholes Bank with Lever Park Avenue. 1999.

Horwich Home Guard at Wallsuches. 1940.

A MISCELLANY OF STREETS AND BY-ROADS

Brownlow Road, Horwich. Circa 1900.

Passageway between Brownlow Road and Albert Street, Horwich. 1967.

Crown Lane, Horwich. Circa 1910. This view was taken from the Crown looking towards Blackrod.

Crown Lane, Horwich. Circa 1910. The opposite view is seen here to the one above with Rivington Pike in the background.

Station Road, Horwich Junction. 1904. This view was taken when looking towards Chorley New Road.

Station Road, Horwich Junction. 1904. A contemporary view to the previous photograph taken when facing towards Blackrod.

Stone Cottages, Bottom o'th Moor, Horwich. 1909.

View of the Squirrel Hotel and Scholes Bank. Circa 1950.

Nelson Street, Horwich showing old weaver's cottages. Circa 1920.

Edge Hill, Horwich. 1912.

Wood Street, Horwich. Circa 1910.

Fox Street, Horwich. Circia 1902.

Mottram Street, Horwich. Circa 1960. This street was named in honour of Julia Catherine Wright of Mottram Hall in Cheshire, who leased the land on which St. Mary's R.C. Church and School were built on Chorley New Road, on the 25th March 1885.

Victoria Road, Horwich. Circa 1920.

The Avenue and Vale House, Horwich. Circa 1910.

Vale Hall, Horwich. 1921.

LIFE'S LITTLE DAY

Ridgmont Cemetery, Horwich. Circa 1920.

On the right is the sculptured Westmacott Statue, erected in Horwich Parish Church in memory of Joseph Ridgway and represents his wife kneeling in prayer.

This interesting old photograph was found during the re-furbishment of premises in Lee Lane, Horwich and shows a burial at Ridgmont Cemetery about 1920. Horwich R.M.I. Band, under their conductor, Mr. Sutcliffe, are providing accompaniment and the number of mourners suggest that a well respected individual is being laid to rest.

Funeral at Ridgmont Cemetery. Circa 1940.

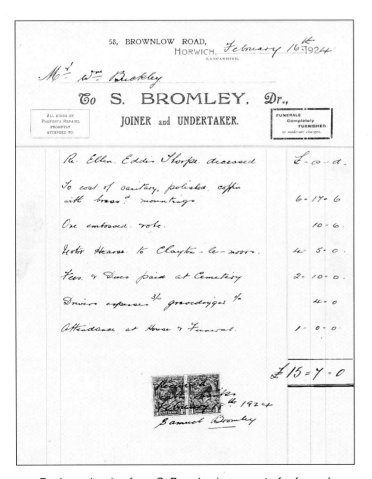

Business invoice from S. Bromley in respect of a funeral.

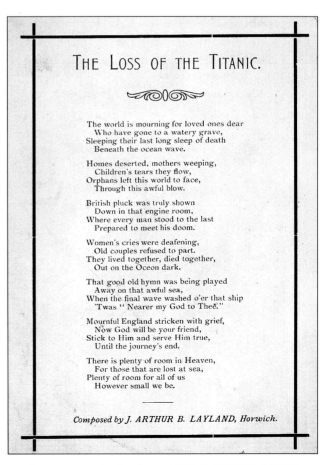

THE LOSS OF THE TITANIC.

The world is mourning for loved ones dear
　Who have gone to a watery grave,
Sleeping their last long sleep of death
　Beneath the ocean wave.

Homes deserted, mothers weeping,
　Children's tears they flow,
Orphans left this world to face,
　Through this awful blow.

British pluck was truly shown
　Down in that engine room,
Where every man stood to the last
　Prepared to meet his doom.

Women's cries were deafening,
　Old couples refused to part.
They lived together, died together,
　Out on the Oceon dark.

That good old hymn was being played
　Away on that awful sea,
When the final wave washed o'er that ship
　'Twas " Nearer my God to Thee."

Mournful England stricken with grief,
　Now God will be your friend,
Stick to Him and serve Him true,
　Until the journey's end.

There is plenty of room in Heaven,
　For those that are lost at sea,
Plenty of room for all of us
　However small we be.

Composed by J. ARTHUR B. LAYLAND, Horwich.

*Poem concerning the loss of R.M.S. TITANIC in 1912,
composed by J. Arthur B. Layland of Horwich.*

APPENDIX 1.

Letter written by James Rothwell, Vicar of Deane Church, Bolton to the Lord Bishop of Chester: -

Bolton, Sept. 21, 1717.

Rev. Sir, - I thought it necessary to send you the following account of Horwich Chapel which I desire you to transmit to my Lord Bishop of Chester. This chapel is three miles distant from the Parish Church (Deane), and the revenue belonging to it is commonly said to be about £9 or £10 per annum, being the interest of about £200 belonging to it, and for a more full proof of this, I here give my following testimony. But in the first place it may be convenient to acquaint you that the chapel has for about this 20 years last past been in the hands of the Dissenters, through the contrivance of the late Lord Willoughby, and the connivance of my predecessor, Richard Hatton, appointed vicar in 1673, who refused to renounce the Covenant, but was, nevertheless, instituted by Bishop Pearson. But when my Lord Bishop of Chester was upon his visitation at Manchester, I acquainted his Lordship with the matter, and his lordship commanded me to give Mr. Walker, the Dissenting teacher, notice to desist, which accordingly I did, and he submitted to his Lordship's commands. Immediately after this I put into the chapel a conformable clergyman, who has supplied the cure ever since, which is above one whole year; and though I gave him the surplice dues of the chapelry, which is all that belongs to me in that part of the Parish, and £2 per annum besides, yet this with his contributions, which is all that he had to subsist on thus far, has not exceeded £14; and when he demanded the interest of the chapel stock during the time of his incumbency, the trustees for the money being Dissenters, tell him they will not pay it till they be forced to do it. Now one of these trustees has told me and several others that the chapel stock is £190 and about two months ago he showed some bonds that were made upon this account, to the sum of about £80. And there are now several living witnesses that can and do testify that the interest of the said chapel stock was paid to Episcopal conforming clergymen that officiated at Horwich Chapel during the reigns of Charles the Second, King James the Second, and until some time after the Revolution; and though this money, as it is said was given to all intents and purposes towards maintaining a curate that should supply the said chapel, yet both against justice and honesty these trustees have sent me word that they will build a meeting house with part of the money, and apply the remaining part towards supporting a Presbyterian teacher. What now is to be done in the affair? I humbly desire my Lord Bishop of Chester's opinion and direction, with your own, - Who am your most humble and most obedient servant, JAMES ROTHWELL. - For the Rev. Dr. Wroe, Warden of Manchester.

APPENDIX 2.

Document for the demolition of the first known chapel at Horwich and the construction of the second.

BEILBY, by Divine permission Lord Bishop of Chester, to all Christian people, to whom these presents (writings) may come, or in anywise appertain, GREETINGS, WHEREAS, we did by a certain instrument in writing under the seal of the office of our then Vicar General and Official Principal, bearing date the eighteenth day of June, in the year of our Lord one thousand seven hundred and seventy-nine, grant a commission or authority to the Reverend Robert Latham, clerk, Vicar of Deane, in the County of Lancaster, and diocese of Chester, the Reverend John Norcross, clerk, curate of Horwich, within the parish of Deane aforesaid, Richard Pilkington the elder, gentleman, Thomas Greenhalgh (since deceased), Robert Etough, William Longworth and Robert Greenhalgh, yeoman, and Hugh Whittle, husbandman, owners of the estates within the chapelry of Horwich aforesaid, who were thereby appointed Commissioners to take down the old Chapel of Horwich aforesaid, and the seats, stalls, and pews therein, and in the room thereof and on part of the yard belonging to the said chapel to erect and build a larger and more handsome and convenient chapel, to contain in length from east to west twenty-two yards and in breadth from north to south twelve yards or thereabouts, and to erect galleries on the north and south sides and at the west end of the said new intended chapel with seats or pews therein, and to allot, appropriate, and dispose of the seats and pews built on the ground below, and in the gallery above, in a fair and equitable manner, first to such as were proprietors of seats in the old chapel in lieu and in full compensation of the seats they were possessed of therein, and to dispose of all other additional seats gained by reconstructing and enlarging of the said chapel, and the uniformity of the seats therein as are on the ground below as in the gallery above, to such of the inhabitants of the said chapelry and others frequenting Divine service in the said chapel as stood in need thereof and would purchase the same at the best prices that would be given for them; and also to enlarge the said chapel yard by taking in part of a field at the east end thereof, belonging to Henry Blundell, Esquire, and by and with his approbation and consent, to contain in length ten yards, and in breadth eight yards or thereabouts; willingly and requiring the said Commissioners as soon as they should have fully executed the said commission to return to us, our Vicar General, or other competent judge, a full certificate thereof, together with a scheme or chart of the seats and pews built and set up in the said new erected chapel, and of their allotment, ordering and disposition of the same, in order to our future approbation and confirmation thereof. AND WHEREAS the aforesaid Reverend Robert Latham, clerk, the Reverend John Norcross, clerk, Robert Etough, William Longworth, Robert Greenhalgh, and Hugh Whittle, six of the survivors of the said commission, have by a certain writing under their hands bearing date in the year of our Lord one thousand seven hundred and eighty-two, duly certified to us that the said chapel hath been by them accordingly re-built with pews and seats therein, and that Divine service is performed therein, and that they had, according to the best of their skill and judgement, and to every information they could procure, allotted, appropriated, and disposed of the seats and pews in the said chapel to and amongst such person and persons as are mentioned in a certain schedule on their part exhibited and deposited in our Consistory Court, who were legally entitled thereunto, and have also returned unto us a scheme or chart of the seats and pews built and set up in the said chapel, and also of the enlargement of the said chapel yard, agreeable to the dimensions aforesaid, and have also certified to us that they had not as yet erected any galleries in the chapel, but have besought us to approve and confirm the allotment and disposition which they have already made, and whereas the Reverend and Worshipful JOHN BRIGGS, clerk, and Master of Arts, our Vicar General and Official Principal, lawfully constituted, right lawfully and judicially proceeding, did enter a general citation or edict, and cause the same, together with the schedule of disposition aforesaid, to be duly published, in time for Divine service in the consecrated chapel of Horwich aforesaid upon Sunday, the first day of September last, thereby inviting all manner of persons in general having or pretending to have any right or title to or interest in the said chapel, or the seats and pews therein, or in the said chapel yard as the same is now enclosed, to appear before our said vicar General and Official Principal, his surrogate, or other deputy judge in that behalf, in the Consistory Court, within the Cathedral Church of Chester upon Thursday, the fifth day of November aforesaid at the hour of hearing causes there, and produce reasonable and lawful cause why the allotment, appropriation, and disposition of the said seats and pews in the said scheme or chart, and particularly described in the schedule aforesaid to the said citation annexed, should not be confirmed to the inhabitants of the said chapelry therein mentioned for the purpose of standing, sitting, preaching or hearing Divine Service, and sermons therein on Sundays and holidays and at all other opportune times, all others excluded without their leave has first been obtained at the instance and promotion of the said Robert Latham, John Norcross, Robert Etough, William Longworth, Robert Greenhalgh, and Hugh Whittle, intimating to all persons so cited as aforesaid, that if they did not appear at the time and place aforesaid, or appearing did not show such a reasonable and lawful cause as aforesaid to the contrary, We, our Vicar General and Official aforesaid, his lawful surrogate, or other competent judge in that behalf, would proceed to approve of and confirm the allotment, appropriation or disposition of the seats and pews to the several and respective persons mentioned in the said schedule for the purposes aforesaid; and likewise to confirm the said chapel yard, so enlarged, to the inhabitants of the said chapelry. AND WHEREAS, upon return of the general citation or edict and praenonization of all persons there judicially made, no person appearing to show cause to the contrary, the Reverend Robert Vanbrugh, clerk, and Master of Arts, lawful surrogate of our Vicar General, and Official Principal aforesaid, rightly, lawfully and judicially proceeding at the petition of the proctor of the said Robert Latham, John Norcross, Robert Etough, William Longworth, Robert Greenhalgh, and Hugh Whittle, did approve of the allotment, appropriation, and disposition aforesaid therein allotted, appropriated, and disposed, and did also decree the aforesaid chapel yard as it is enlarged, enclosed, and described in the said scheme or chart now remaining in the Publick (sic) Episcopal Registry of our diocese, to be confirmed to and for the use of the inhabitants of the said chapelry as by the act of Court in that behalf made on Thursday, the fifth day of November last, reference thereunto being had, may appear. KNOW YE therefore that we the said BEILBY, Lord Bishop of Chester, have approved of and confirmed, and by these presents do approve of and confirm the aforesaid new erection, and the allotment, appropriation, and disposition of the seats and pews and sitting places built and set up, and as they are numbered and described in the schedule hereunto annexed and described in the scheme or chart aforesaid, and remaining in our Public Episcopal Registry aforesaid; and we do likewise (as far as in us lies) confirm the aforesaid chapel yard as it is now enlarged, enclosed, and described in the scheme or chart aforesaid unto and to the use of the inhabitants of the said chapelry, for the purpose of burying the dead therein; and do also (as far as in us lies), and by the law we now confirm the respective seats, pews and sitting places within the said chapel to the several persons mentioned in the schedule and scheme or chart aforesaid, to whom they thereby appear to have been allotted, appropriated, and disposed of to and for the uses of standing, sitting, kneeling, or hearing Divine service and sermons therein on Sundays and holidays and at all other appropriate times by themselves, their families, or tenants so long as they shall continue to resort to Divine service in the said chapel, all others excluded without their leave first had and obtained and the ordinary right and jurisdiction of us and all our successors in all the seats, pews, and sitting places within the said chapel, and also in the yard of the said chapel being always hereafter saved and reserved; IN TESTIMONY Whereof we have caused these Letters Testimonial to be made and the seal of the office of our Vicar General and Official Principal aforesaid, which we use in this behalf to be put hereto.

Given at Chester the eighth day of May, in the year of our Lord one thousand seven hundred (the remainder of the date has been cut off the document). This agrees with the Decree of Court, Hugh Speed, Deputy Registrar.

As set forth in the text above there is annexed to the faculty the subjoined "account of the seats in Horwich Chapel, to what lands they belong, who the owners of the lands are, and the names of the tenants or occupiers, with the number of seats belonging to each as allotted and appointed by the Commissioners under a faculty, 1782":-

NO.	LANDS	OWNERS	TENANTS OR OCCUPIERS	SITTINGS
1	Roscoe's	Hy. Blundell, Esq.	Gabriel Pilkington	4
	Greenhough's	Mr. Greenhough	Wm. Butterworth	2
2	Part of			
	Makinson's	Mr. Thos Scott	James Grundy	2
3	Hodgkinson's	Rev. H. Offley Wright	John Hodgkinson	4
			John Hopwood	4
4	Knowles's	Mr. R. Pilkington	John Turner	2
5	Walker Fold	Miss Byrom	James Scolfield	2
6	Wilson Fold	Hy. Blundell, Esq.	Wm. Kirkman	4
			P. Vause &	4
			J. Longworth	
7	Dakin's	Robert Etough	Robt. Tong, &c	4
8	Pendlebury's	Hy. Blundell, Esq.	Robert Pendlebury	4
9	Whittle's	Rev. H. Offley Wright	Mr. Peter Gorton	2
	Makinson's	Evan Makinson	Robert Pendlebury	2
10-11	Boardman's	Mrs. Wright	Thomas Scolfield	8
12	Markland's	Richard Mason	Richard Mason	4
13	Gills,		Robert Etough	2
	Whittle's and			
	Hugh Whittle			2
	Stocks	Hy. Blundell, Esq.	Rd. Pilkington and	2
			John Etough	2
			Hugh Makinson	2

No.				
14	Horrock's	Jane Marsden	Thomas Kershaw	2
	Peake's and	John Knowles and	Jas. Turner and	
	Knuston's	Jas. Lomax	Jas. Smith	2
		Rev. H. Offley	Rich. Brownlow	
		Wright	and J. Kershaw	4
15	Makinson's	- Boardman	Wm. Longworth	4
	Markland's	John Mason	John Mason	4
16	Lostock Hall	Hy. Blundell, Esq.	Jas Shaw & others	8
17	Wallsuch	Hy. Blundell, Esq.	Mr. Thos. Ridgway	4
		Mr. Thos Ridgway		4
18	Horwich Chapel	The Curate of	Rich. Worthington	8
	Land	Horwich		19
		Mr. R. Greenhalgh		4
20		Wm. Longworth		4
21		Robt. Pendlebury		4
22		Hugh Whittle		4
23		Harry Stones		4
24		James Scowcroft		4
25		Widow Worthington		4
26		Rob. Sharples		4
27		Mr. Thos Ridgway		4
28-31		The Singers		1
32	Scholes Bank	Rev. H. Offley Wright	Mary Stones	4
33		Rich. Brownlow		4
34		John Etough		4
35	Greenhalgh's	Mr. Thos. Nuttall	Mr. Jas. Eckersley	4
36	Part of late	Mr. Richard Pilkington		1
	Bolton's			
	Peel Chapel			
	Lands	Peel Chapel		3
37	Walker Fold	Wm. Longworth	Wm. Longworth	4
38	Pilkington's			
	Mr. Rich. Pilkington			2
	and Knowles's	Hy. Blundell, Esq.	Snr, William Thornley	2
39	Coleman's	Mr. R. Greenhalgh	Mr. R. Greenhalgh	4
40	Gorton's		Mr. Peter Gorton	4
	and Mather's		Rt. Pendlebury, Hilton,	
			and Pet. Longworth	
41	Old Lord's	Rev. H. Offley	Mr. Nightingale	4
	Hilton's	Wright	Mr. Peter Gorton	4
42	Walton's		Mr. Charter's	4
	Dr. Anderton's		Mr. Hy. Pilkington	4
43		James Stones		3

Signed: -
R. Latham, Vicar
John Norcross, Curate of Horwich.
Robt. Greenhalgh
Robert Eatough
William Longworth
Hugh Whittle

APPENDIX 3

The following are extracts from the will of the late Mr. Joseph Ridgway, who died at Leamington on the 26th day of June, 1842, but they relate only to his donations and bequests to the Incumbent and officers of Horwich Church and other persons residing in the township: -

I desire to be buried in my vault at the church in Horwich, and I direct my executors to erect a monument in the same church to my memory, to be executed by a London artist, at such expense as they, my executors, may think proper, but not less than £1000; also a tablet recording the benefactions which I may have made by this my will, or otherwise, to the said church, and the officers thereof, so that the said benefactions may not be lost for want of due notice of their proper application. I direct my executors to procure and set up a clock face on each of the east, west, and north sides of the tower of the church in Horwich aforesaid, corresponding in appearing with the clock face already set up in the south side thereof, with proper works for showing the time at each of the said faces, and for striking or telling the quarters of the hour.

I direct my executors to set apart and invest in Three Per Centum Consolidated or Reduced Bank Annuities a sum producing the clear yearly income of £132, free from legacy duty, commencing from the end of one year, from the time when the Reverend David Hewitt, now Incumbent Minister of the church at Horwich aforesaid, shall have ceased to be such Incumbent Minister; but if such one year shall expire during my life, then commencing from the time of my decease.

And I direct the said yearly income of £132 to be paid to and at the discretion of the minister and wardens of the church at Horwich aforesaid, for the time being, and my trustees and executors hereinafter named, or the trustees acting in their place, under this my will for the time being, or such of the said several persons as may from time to time attend and be present as follow, videlicit: -

Forty pounds a year, part thereof as a salary for the organist of the same church for ever.

Thirty pounds a year, further part thereof to pay the singers or choir of the same church for ever.

Twenty-four pounds a year, further part thereof to pay the ringers of the bells of the same church for ever.

Sixteen pounds a year, further part thereof to provide and furnish the clerk of the same church for ever with a gown and habilaments, like those worn by the clerk for the church for the blind at Liverpool, and the remainder of the said £16 as a perpetual salary for the same clerk of the church at Horwich, but for which he is to clean and take care of the tablet and monument hereinafter directed.

Twelve pounds a year, further part thereof to provide and furnish the beadle of the same church forever with a gown and habilaments like those worn by the beadle for the church for the blind at Liverpool aforesaid, and the remainder of the said £12 a year as a perpetual salary for the beadle of the same church at Horwich aforesaid.

And ten pounds a year, residue thereof as a salary for the organ blower for the same church at Horwich for ever.

I further direct my executors to invest as aforesaid a sum producing a yearly income of £10, free from legacy duty, commencing from the time of my decease, to be paid and applied by my trustees, and executors hereinafter named, or the trustees acting in their place, under this my will for the time being, during the incumbency of the said David Hewitt, as a salary for the person as shall wind up and regulate the clock of the same church at Horwich, and who shall also ring one of the bells in the tower at the hours of 6 in the morning and 8 in the evening for the space of fifteen minutes, and after determination of such incumbency of the said David Hewitt then I direct the said income of £10 a year to be paid by and at the discretion of the said minister and wardens all for the time being, and my trustees and executors hereinafter named, or the trustees acting in their place under this my will for the time being, or such of the said several persons as may from time to time attend and be present as a salary for such clock winder and regulator and ringer as aforesaid for ever.

And I request that Mr. Rollinson, who is now employed as ringer of the said bell at six and eight o'clock, may continue to be so employed, and hold that situation during his life.

And from and after the determination of the said incumbency of the said David Hewitt,

I direct my executors to provide, at the expense of my estate a service of communion plate for the use of Horwich Church aforesaid, the same to be massive and embossed with an inscription, and my armorial bearings thereon, also a virge, or sceptre, of silver, to be carried before the minister of the same church from the vestry to the reading desk and pulpit; and a full suit of canonicals for the first and next Incumbent of Horwich aforesaid other than the said David Hewitt.

And I direct the legacy tax upon these bequests of communion service, virge, or sceptre, and canonicals to be paid out of my estate.

And from and after the decease or marriage again of my said wife,

I direct my executors to set apart and invest in three per centum consolidated or reduced bank annuities, a sum producing a yearly income of £100, free from legacy tax, and commencing from the death or marriage again of my said wife (unless I survive her, and then from the time of my decease).

And I direct the said income of £100 a year to be applied as part of the annual produce of my residuary personal estate until the said David Hewitt shall have ceased to be the Incumbent Minister of Horwich Church, and from and after the death or marriage again of my wife and the said David Hewitt ceasing to be such Incumbent Minister, then the said yearly income of £100 to be added unto and become part of the salary, stipend, or living of the Incumbent Minister of the same Church at Horwich.

Provided that in case the present or any future Vicar of Deane shall take or hold the said curacy, living, or incumbency of Horwich, or if the said David Hewitt shall ever hereafter take or hold the same, then during all such tenure or holding the said payment and application of the said yearly income of £100 to the purpose aforesaid, shall be suspended, and the same income during all such time be applied as part of the yearly produce of my residuary personal estate.

And from and after the decease or marriage again of my wife, I direct my executors to set apart and invest in three per centum of consolidated or reduced bank annuities a sum producing a clear income of £150 a year, free from legacy tax, and commencing from the death or marriage again of my said wife, unless I survive her, and then from the time of my own decease, to be paid and applied as follows, that is to say;

Fifty pounds, part thereof, to be paid and applied at the discretion of the minister and wardens of the same church at Horwich for the time being, and of my trustees and executors hereinafter named, or the trustees acting in their place, all for the time being, or such of the said persons as may, from time to time, attend and be present as a salary for the master of the school at the east end of the same church, which master shall be a member of the Established Church of England, and for which salary he shall instruct in reading and writing 40 poor children of the township of Horwich, the same children to be nominated by and at the discretion of the said minister and churchwardens of the township of Horwich aforesaid, all for the time being, and of my trustees and executors hereinafter named, or the trustees acting in their place under this my will or the time being, or such of the said several persons as may from time to time attend and be present.

One hundred pounds a year, being the residue thereof, to be applied by and at the discretion of the said minister and wardens for the time being, and my trustees and executors hereinafter named, or the trustees acting in their place under this my will for the time being, or such of the said several persons as may from time to time attend and be present in the purchase of clothing and bedding for the poor inhabitants of Horwich, to be distributed at or soon after Old Michaelmas Day in each year, and in such distribution I wish the oldest and poorest inhabitants of Horwich who have been most regular in their attendance at church on Sundays to be preferred, regard nevertheless being had to such as from sickness or old age are unable to attend.

I further direct that if the sum of £400 can be raised by subscription or otherwise within one year after my decease and the death or marriage again of my said wife, to build or provide a parsonage house for the residence of the Incumbent Minister of the church at Horwich aforesaid, then my executors do and shall after the death or marriage again of my said wife, which ever shall first happen, subscribe and pay from such part of my estate as may be legally bequeathed, or given by will to that purpose, the sum of £800, free from legacy duty, with interest from the time of my death, and the death or marriage again of my said wife, until actual payment, but unless £400 can be so raised by subscription or otherwise, this legacy of £800 is to lapse, and sink into the residue of my estate.

The trustees appointed by the will were John Woodhouse, Esq., gentleman, and John Mangnall, Esq., paper manufacturer, both of Bolton, together with the testator's wife Anna Maria Ridgway. The present trustees are Thomas Lever Rushton, Esq., of Moor Platt, Horwich, and William Howarth Esq., Wallsuches, Horwich. The will was proved at Chester on the 25th of January 1843.

In addition to the benefactions above named, Mr. Joseph Ridgway bequeathed the following amounts to the institutions named: -

For building, enlarging, or improving a school in the borough of Bolton, under the rules and regulations of the National Education Society £2000
To the Bolton Infirmary and Dispensary 1000
To the Schoolmaster at the intended new school at Bolton (annually). 100
To the Society for building churches in the diocese of Chester 1000
To the widows and orphans of clergymen within the Archdeaconry of Chester 500
Society for the Propagation of the Gospel 500
Society for Promoting Christian Knowledge 500
National Society for Promoting the Education of the Poor 200
Manchester School for the Blind 200
Manchester School for the Deaf and Dumb 200
Manchester Infirmary 200
School for the Blind, Liverpool 500
Blue Coat School, Liverpool 200
Liverpool Deaf and Dumb School 200
Collegiate Institution, Liverpool 200
Additional Curates' Society 200
Sons of Clergy Society 200

These bequests became available on the death of Mrs. Ridgway, which took place on the 14th of November, 1860, at Hatton Hall, Northamptonshire. The first distribution of clothing, &c., to the poor of Horwich as prescribed for in the will took place of the 6th January, 1862. One of the bells of the church, for the ringing of which Mr. Ridgway left an annual sum, is regularly rung for a quarter of an hour at quarter before 6 o'clock in the morning, and at eight in the evening. It is called the six and eight o'clock bell, and in the morning especially is of great service to that portion of the working population whose avocation compels them to rise at a rather early hour. Amongst the above bequests it will be seen that Mr. Ridgway left £800 with interest towards erecting on the decease of his widow a vicarage at Horwich, provided that within a year of her decease the sum of £400 could otherwise be raised to augment the benefaction. This latter sum was forthcoming within the prescribed time for the Rev. H. S. Pigot and Mrs. Pigot subscribed towards it £125. Mrs. Pigot obtained from her private friends another £100, and the remainder was prescribed by parishioners and friends. The vicarage is charmingly situated upon an elevated site, and commands a view from the front of a level wooded expanse of country, with the sea and mountain scenery in the back-ground; indeed, few could imagine that within such a short distance of the smoke of Bolton such a delightful view of landscape, mountain, and marine scenery can be obtained.

OLD HORWICH

Water colour depicting Gorton Fold, Horwich, in 1825.

Painting of Washpool, Horwich, by George H. Simms. 1922.

VIEWS ABOUT THE TOWN

View across Park Reservoir, Chorley Old Road, Horwich, with Rivington Pike in the background and Wallsuches chimney on the left.

This photograph was taken prior to the development of Stocks Park Estate. Horwich Parish Church can be seen far right.

Local steeplejack Fred Dibnah carried out maintenance on Horwich Parish Church tower during the 1990's.

Horwich Leisure Centre, Victoria Road / Church Street, Horwich.

THE CHANGING ORDER

Lee Lane Chapel was demolished during the 1980's and Chapel's Restaurant was constructed on the site. These photographs were taken during the building process.

The Tesco Supermarket at Horwich is to be re-sited in the near future and the present site will be occupied by Fort James (U.K) Ltd.

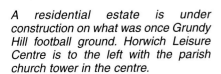

The Mill and the Granary, which is the property in the foreground, was once known as Crowther Fold Mill.

A residential estate is under construction on what was once Grundy Hill football ground. Horwich Leisure Centre is to the left with the parish church tower in the centre.

THE NEW MIDDLEBROOK RETAIL
AND LEISURE PARK DEVELOPMENT

View of Horwich from the M.61 link-road prior to the development at Middlebrook.

Development of the new Middlebrook Retail and Leisure Park represented an investment of £150 million by Orbit Developments, a member of the Emerson Group. Construction of the 200 acre scheme commenced in January 1997 and created approximately 3,000 jobs. The Holiday Inn Express (shown above under construction) contains 74 bedrooms and is situated close to licensed premises - Bennigans and Innkeepers Fayre.

Construction of the Bolton Wanderers Football Club Stadium at Middlebrook. 1996.

The new stadium almost complete. 1997.

FINAL ASPECTS

Rockhaven, Horwich, from Brownlow Road. painted by G. H. Simms 1926.

This aerial view of the Red Moss at Horwich, photographed by R. A. Shires, was sold on post cards to aid the group working for protection, enhancement and conservation of the peat bog habitat. Its aims were largely successful.